Peter,

MANDELA

Other books by Ronald Harwood

Novels
All the Same Shadows
The Guilt Merchants
The Girl in Melanie Klein
Articles of Faith
The Genoa Ferry
Cesar and Augusta

Short Stories
One. Interior. Day. Adventures in the Film Trade

Biography
Sir Donald Wolfit CBE: His Life and Work in the
Unfashionable Theatre

Plays
A Family
The Ordeal of Gilbert Pinfold (from Evelyn Waugh)
The Dresser
After the Lions
Tramway Road
The Deliberate Death of a Polish Priest
Interpreters

Miscellaneous
A Night at the Theatre (Editor)
The Ages of Gielgud (Editor)
All the World's a Stage

Ronald Harwood

MANDELA

First published in 1987 by Boxtree Limited

Text © Ronald Harwood

ISBN 1 85283 204 5

Printed and bound in Great Britain by
Butler & Tanner Ltd, Frome and London
for Boxtree Limited
25 Floral Street
London WC2E 9DS

CONTENTS

ACKNOWLEDGEMENTS

I should like to acknowledge the individuals and organisations, who wish to remain anonymous, and who gave so freely of their time and knowledge. I must also mention those countless cameramen and journalists who provided invaluable documentary footage which proved to be one of the main sources of information, especially when writing the screenplay.

The film of *Mandela* is a TVS production in association with Titus Productions.

Screenplay..............................Ronald Harwood
Producer..................................Dickie Bamber
Executive Producers...............Robert Berger and Herbert Brodkin
Director...................................Philip Saville
Composer................................Richard Hartley

CAST LIST

Nelson Mandela......................Danny Glover
Winnie Mandela......................Alfre Woodard
Walter Sisulu..........................John Matshikiza
Oliver Tambo..........................John Indi
Swanepoel...............................Warren Clarke
Albert Luthuli.........................Nathan Dambusa Moledle
Zindzi Mandela.......................Soliswa Sithole

Photos of Danny Glover used by permission of Danny Glover. Photos of Alfre Woodard used by permission of Alfre Woodard.

LIST OF ILLUSTRATIONS

The author and publishers would like to thank the following for
permission to reproduce photographs:

Photos 1, 2, 9–11, 12, 14, 25: Eli Weinberg/IDAF. Photos 8, 21,
27, 28, 33, 34, 39, 41, 43, 44: IDAF. Photo 3: Jurgen Schadeberg.
Photo 17: Ian Berry/Camera Press. Photos 40, 42: Peter
Magubane/IDAF. Photo 45: Sam Nzima/Argus. Photo 48: Morris
Zwi.

Photos 4–7, 13, 15, 16, 18, 19, 20, 22–24, 26, 29–32, 35–38, 46,
47 by Tony Nutley from the film *Mandela*, TVS.

INTRODUCTION

This book is intended as an accompaniment to the film for which I also wrote the screenplay. Although in many respects one reflects the other, the approach to each is entirely different.

The film is a dramatised account of Nelson Mandela's life since 1952. In order to compress such a great sweep of events into the space of two-and-a-half hours a good deal of telescoping, simplification, compression and cinematic shorthand was necessary. Furthermore, I wanted in the screenplay to balance Mandela's political activities with his private life. I was drawn to this shape because of the remarkable qualities of Winnie Mandela, the woman with whom he fell in love and later married. The film, then, not only seeks to tell the story of the Mandelas' fight against apartheid, but also attempts to reveal something of the extraordinary bond between the man and the woman, a bond which sustained them through their struggle against a brutal and inhuman social system.

I have not, in the pages of this book, tried to present a conventional biography. There would be no point, since a first-class account of his life and times, *Nelson Mandela, The Man and the Movement*, by Mary Benson already exists. Instead, I have followed the path of the screenplay but have given much more historical, political and social background than is ever possible in a film. I have also punctuated the narrative with extracts from the screenplay in the hope of giving the reader some flavour of the film and, perhaps, some insight into my method as a dramatist.

Ronald Harwood
London, 1987

To my cousin, Bruce Evans, Bishop of Port Elizabeth

PART ONE

INHERITANCE

1

BLACK AND WHITE

The life of Nelson Mandela has come to symbolise the struggle for justice and freedom in South Africa because it contains the essential element of an epic story, which is that the experience of one man represents and reinforces the experience of many. History is alive with these human symbols who, by acting as a kind of lens, help us to focus on complex motives and events which might otherwise remain blurred. All epics, in fact and fiction, seek to make a vast collective conflict intelligible in terms of one central figure or group. Nelson Mandela is such a figure. The danger of oversimplifying or inadvertently diminishing the contributions of others is offset by the privilege of hearing an individual voice which speaks loudly, clearly and often movingly for millions.

In contrast to the tumult that was later to surround him, Nelson Rolihlahla Mandela's life began in pastoral tranquillity. He was born on 18 July 1918 at Qunu near Umtata in the Transkei, an area which lies roughly between East London and Durban on the southeastern seaboard of the subcontinent and is now the designated 'homeland' of the Xhosa people. His father, Henry Gadla Mandela, was a minor chief of the Tembu and had four wives; one of them, Nelson's mother, Nonqaphi, was apparently a considerable personality. Both parents were unschooled in the formal sense but, as members of the royal family, followed subtle, secure and ancient traditions. They gave their son two names. The first, Nelson, reflects the British colonial influence; the second, his Xhosa name, Rolihlahla, was prophetic: it means 'stirring up trouble'.

Because of his royal background, Nelson was born with the expectation of leadership which, in turn, entails responsibility. Loyalty to the chief is the first essential of the Xhosa code of honour. In return the chief dispenses justice and ensures order. Nelson's father, Henry, was the leading counsellor to the Paramount Chief of the Tembu, to whom he was related. Together they had joined the South African army to fight the Germans in Southwest Africa, now Namibia, in the First World War. He also served on the

Transkeian Territories General Council – the *Bunga* – which advised the Pretoria government on local matters and was made up of Africans and Europeans. Service to the community, therefore, was an important part of Nelson's heritage.

The Xhosa are a sociable, gregarious people, renowned for their hospitality; travellers will always be assured of a meal and a place to sleep. In Qunu, as elsewhere, the *kraal* of white-washed huts was the centre of community life; beyond were maize fields, and cattle grazing near the Mbashe River. In this peaceful, protected environment Nelson grew up. By day, there would be a farmer's work for him to learn and he helped with the ploughing of the fields. At night, around a great open fire, it was his imagination which was stimulated. In his only autobiographical note, he wrote:

> My political interest was first aroused when I listened to elders of our tribe in my village as a youth. They spoke of the good old days before the arrival of the White Man. Our people lived peacefully under the democratic rule of their Kings and Counsellors and moved freely all over their country. Then the country was ours. We occupied the land, the forests and the rivers. We set up and operated our own Government; we controlled our own armies, and organised our own trade and commerce.

There were too the tales of former glories, of great heroes like Hintsa and Makanda, of a more fulfilling, free and independent life before the coming of the white man.

By the time of his birth, the white man had made his presence felt in southern Africa for just over 250 years. The conflict in which Nelson was to be a principal protagonist began the moment the first Dutch settlers set foot on the Cape of Good Hope. What did they encounter, those adventurers from Holland? From their ships they would have seen a vista of almost unparalleled beauty, what an earlier traveller, Francis Drake, called 'the fairest cape in all the world', a diadem of mountains, two peaks either side an almost perfect table. Under the intense blue of the sky, the mountains appear pearl-grey, and the land is green and lush. They came in April, when the heat of summer had passed, but even so they would have found it warm in comparison to the autumn of northern Europe. If they judged the weather kind they must also have been pleasantly surprised to find a natural bay where they could safely drop anchor and which protected their ships from the unpredictable and often violent moods of the Atlantic Ocean. The leader of the expedition was Jan Van Riebeeck and he had under his command 90 men. All were employed by the Dutch East India Company with precise instructions to do nothing more than establish at the Cape a half-way house, a small revictualling station for the Company's ships on their way to and from the East Indies.

Van Riebeeck was rowed ashore on 6 April 1652 and he soon discovered that he and his men were not the only human beings about: small, yellowy-brown men with tight peppercorn hair came down from the mountain slopes to greet the newcomers, for they had seen Europeans before – earlier Portuguese explorers and sailors who had stopped to trade – and so were not unduly alarmed. These people were the Khoikhoi, whom the Dutchmen called Hottentots.

The inevitable conflict was not long in coming. Van Riebeeck and his party began building a fort, set up a small hospital for sick sailors and grew vegetables on the slopes of Table Mountain. But because the Dutch East India Company wanted to make their new half-way house self-supporting, Van Riebeeck was instructed to supply not only the fresh fruit, vegetables and cereals to the Company's ships, but also dairy produce and meat. The vegetable garden was soon established and to begin with proved adequate for the station's needs; the problem arose when it came to dairy produce and meat: for these commodities, cattle were needed and the Khoikhoi had cattle. For a while they bartered with the Europeans, but soon began to resist. Within seven years of Van Riebeeck's arrival the first Khoikhoi–Dutch War erupted. The Khoikhoi had greater numbers but the Dutch had guns and cunning; the war ended in stalemate. The Company promised to respect the Khoikhoi's rights and the Khoikhoi agreed to cease their harassment of the settlers. The pattern had been set. The white man had gained a foot-hold on the Cape peninsula; his craving to take steps further afield now dominates this history.

In less than a hundred years the settlement had grown into a colony. So distant from head office in the Netherlands, the Cape grew into an autonomous subsidiary. Corruption was rife. The government, hypocritically claiming legitimacy from Holland, was run by Company employees who lined their own pockets, farmed privately and illegally, and sought preferential treatment in all matters fiscal. This did not endear them to those they governed, the *burghers* of the colony. By the end of the eighteenth century there were reputedly only ten law books in the Cape and the local joke was that no one had ever read them. It was easier for officials to make up the ordinances as they went along. The colony was wild, uncontrolled and lawless. What discipline there was seems to have been administered by the Dutch Reformed Church, harsh, fundamentalist, preaching Divine Will in return for obedience and doubtful morality. There were also 25,000 slaves serving 20,000 colonists. The Khoikhoi had been decimated and a new race was in the process of being created: the Coloured people, neither black nor white but a mixture, a result of impulses more human perhaps than colonial.

The colonists took little interest in the world outside. Their concerns were local, their motives selfish and acquisitive. The *burghers* pushed north and east, and thus encountered new peoples, notably the Xhosa, the black farmers of the Eastern Cape. At first, the Xhosa were friendly, but cattle-rustling ensued, and there were disputes over hunting and grazing rights. The Cape government tried to intervene by prohibiting white settlements in the area; the *burghers* resisted. This, too, set a pattern for the future. The white settlers resented any interference in their affairs and responded in two ways: they tried open defiance either by ignoring the edicts and instructions, or, in some isolated incidents, by setting up small 'republics'; if that did not work, they simply moved further away, out of reach. By then the white frontiersmen were called *Boers*, which in Dutch means 'farmers'; these journeys that a small number undertook were called *treks*.

Enter the British. In 1795, the House of Orange, which had ruled the Netherlands, was overthrown. William of Orange found asylum in England and asked his hosts to seize control of the Cape on his behalf. They obliged. Their first occupation was brief because in 1803, under the Treaty of Amiens, the Cape was handed back to the Netherlands. But by the time the British were spoiling for their fight with Napoleon, they had realised the strategic importance of the Cape in relation to India. In 1806 they again took possession of the colony; in 1815, at the end of the Napoleonic wars, their presence was confirmed by international law.

No self-respecting dramatist would dream of creating protagonists as wildly different as the British ruling class and the Boers they had now to govern. The British: mostly upper-class, well-educated, ex-India hands, members of the Church of England which regarded God as a kindly old Etonian and which Disraeli was to call 'the Conservative Party at prayer'. The Boers: rough-hewn, dour, resentful of authority, adherents of an austere Christian faith owing its allegiance it seemed to Jehovah rather than Jesus. The conflict was inevitable and cruel.

The British, regarding the Cape as a profitable little outpost, hoped for a quiet and prosperous life. But the Boers on the eastern frontier were, as ever, insensitive to the wishes of their rulers. The British, enthused by the sentiment of emancipating slaves, threatened their livelihood. The Boers continued to annex new territory and to engage in violent disputes with the Xhosa. The British tried everything to keep control. They decided that blacks and whites should be kept apart and introduced buffer zones between the two communities; but then, because business was their business, they instituted trade fairs to which blacks were welcomed. Borrowing a system from the old Dutch East India Company, the British revitalised the 'pass' system, which regulated the movement of blacks and helped to lay the foundation of a hated and persistent device. Thus the policy of separation was rendered useless by the shopkeepers' mentality. Recognising cheap labour when they saw it, the British also encouraged blacks to work for whites on their farms and in their houses. Yet the British, at the centre of a world trading empire, believed in market forces and that meant a free exchange of ideas, goods, labour. This was the Whig mentality at its best, which brought in its wake the English missionaries, Christian soldiers marching as to war. Under their influence codes of conduct were instituted: for example, blacks were not to be put in chains nor were they to be chastised except after a fair trial. To the Boers on the frontier, any notion of regulating their way of life was anathema. In their eyes the non-whites were hewers of wood and carriers of water who were needed to perform those services for their white masters. They had, therefore, to be controlled. Free them, cried the missionaries, all men are equal in the sight of God. Can't we find a compromise, asked the British government, resorting to a well-tried and favoured approach. It was a head-on clash between colonial paternalism, religious fervour and brutal feudalism. Feudalism won.

Since they were unable to bring stability to the eastern frontier by law, persuasion or force of arms, the British decided on a policy of immigration. In 1820, English families were lured to the Cape by the promise of free passage and, on arrival, a parcel of land in the Eastern Cape. These were to be the founding fathers of the English-speaking population. Unwittingly, the government had added another irreconcilable ingredient to what they must have hoped would be a melting-pot for black, white, Briton, Boer, Khoikhoi, Coloureds, languages, cultures, aspirations, creeds. They were to be sorely disappointed. The Boers shunned the British and in a great surge moved further and further north, a migration that was to be known as the Great Trek. The British did their best to pursue them and bring them under the rule of law.

For most of the nineteenth century this struggle continued. The Boers' ally was geography, the vast hinterland, bounded in the east by the Indian Ocean, but seemingly unending across the Orange River, north towards the Vaal and Limpopo. Undertaking journeys of great hardship, the *Voortrekkers*, the folk heroes of their descendants, gave up the security and comfort of permanent settlements to escape British rule, such was the extent of their dissatisfaction. The British, however, were not the only enemy. The *Voortrekkers* reached into what is today the Orange Free State; after a dispute as to what direction they should take next, they turned east to Natal. There, in February 1838, they encountered the might of the Zulus under their king, Dingane. The king invited them to watch a ceremonial dance in the royal *kraal* at Mgungundhlovu. At an appropriate moment he gave a signal to his warriors. The party of Boers was slaughtered. By the end of the year, learning of a planned full-scale Zulu attack, the Boers employed a favourite tactic: they formed their covered wagons in a circle which they called a *laager* and waited for the onslaught. On 16 December, a terrible battle took place by the Ncome River. The Zulus were beaten off: so fierce was the fighting that the river literally ran red with Zulu blood. The betrayal by Dingane, the *laager*, the Battle of Blood River entered the Boers' psyche and to this day are some of the most powerful elements in their collective memory.

But the Boers had won and so set up the Boer Republic which the British were not disposed to recognise. The British had a highly-trained army and the imperial will on their side. By annexing Natal they tried to bring the wayward Boers under control. But the Boers had trekked hundreds of miles precisely to be rid of the British. Now, after all they had gone through, was there nothing to be done except submit? Their answer was to inspan the ox wagons and return to the Orange Free State or go even further afield across the Vaal River. But the British would not easily give up these recalcitrant colonists, who were, under a law passed in faraway Cape Town, still British subjects. There was no alternative to the ruling power but to move in on the Free State. Some Boer leaders accepted their fate. Others, trying a statesmanlike approach, decided to negotiate, which proved more successful. By the Sand River Convention of 1852, the British agreed that the Boers in the Transvaal should have independence. So came into being the South African Republic. Seeing how well this worked, the British, two years later, gave similar independence to the Orange Free State. The Boers had succeeded in establishing themselves in two autonomous regions.

For a short while there was a precarious balance between the warring elements, black and white, Boer and Briton. The Boers had won battles over some black armies and had found a place in the sun. Then, children at play ruined it all. Wanting a marble to use in their game, a group of them near a place called Kimberley found in the desert sands a shiny stone. The stone turned out to be a diamond of magnificent quality and there were more, many more, to be unearthed. Now, the question arose, who owned the diamond fields? Six years after the first discovery, and after many claims and counter-claims, the British paid £90,000 compensation to the Orange Free State and took possession of the area which, in 1880, was incorporated in the Cape Colony. 'This is the rock', said a British Colonial Secretary, holding up one of the larger finds, 'on which the future success of South Africa will be built.' Predictably, British interest in the rest of the country was quickened. Attempts to federate and then to conquer the Boer republics were initiated. By embarking on this course, the British had also to contend with one of the greatest fighting machines in Africa: the Zulus. After a savage defeat at Isandhlwana and a Pyrrhic victory at Rorke's Drift, the British retaliated. On 4 July 1879 they decisively routed the Zulu army at Ulundi.

The British were soon in control of the Transvaal and had brought the Boers of the South African Republic back under their control; but by inflicting so great a defeat on the Zulus, and later, on the other powerful army of the Pedi in the Eastern Transvaal, they had inadvertently altered the balance of power. For no longer had blacks the military might to resist the Boers. This was to contribute in no small way to the violence in the years to come.

And then there was gold. In 1885, on the Witwatersrand, the first nuggets were discovered. Soon, as the digging and prospecting got underway, it became clear that, by comparison, diamonds were literally child's play. A great reef, more or less surrounding Johannesburg, contained vast deposits of gold not quite beyond the dreams of avarice. From all over the world, the hopeful descended on the Transvaal. The foreigners were called *uitlanders* and in the space of less than fifteen years they outnumbered the resident Boer population. While this may have worried the Boers, led by Paul Kruger, it was of less concern to the British. What interested them was the fabulous wealth that lay just beyond their grasp. An unscrupulous but brilliant adventurer, Cecil John Rhodes, had a vision of a British continent from Cape to Cairo but with motives that were double-edged. His imperial ambitions were limitless; so too was his greed. Financially daring, politically shrewd, he manoeuvred and manipulated and finally engineered the collision he knew was both inevitable and, from his point of view, desirable. In October 1899 what has come to be called the Boer War erupted. The British took on the combined Boer forces of the Transvaal and the Orange Free State.

It lasted three years and the British were the victors. When the peace was finally signed at Vereeniging on 31 May 1902, it was the end of the armed struggle but the conflict remained for the next half-century, the Boers resentful of the political dominance of English-speakers inside the country. The Transvaal and Orange Free State became British colonies, but the Boers were promised limited self-government; Dutch was guaranteed as the second official language after English. But Dutch itself would soon give way to the *lingua franca* of the Boers, a kind of *patois*, kitchen-Dutch, called Afrikaans. And although the Boers soon realised they formed the majority of the white population and would perhaps be able to deal politically with undue British influence, there was another factor to be considered. The Boers, because they had fought a common enemy spread over a large geographical area, now felt they had at last achieved a national, spiritual identity. This sense of unity, of *volk*, of Afrikanerdom, was to be their inspiration in the twentieth century.

The British plan was to unify the four colonies: the Cape, Natal, Transvaal and Orange Free State. On 31 May 1910 the Union of South Africa came into being, a self-governing dominion of the British Empire. The British, who for so long had fought for control, now in effect withdrew. The blacks took no part in any of these arrangements. They were regarded, to a lesser or greater degree, as a subject people. The economics of racism was to be the dominant factor in the future. Arguments will rage as to what produced the dreadful injustices of modern South Africa. The materialist, pragmatic view will lean towards the economic argument: racism was inevitable if maximum benefit was to be obtained from the country's great mineral wealth. The Boers, with British help, had subdued the black nations by force of arms. From north to south there was a cowed, ready-made workforce of cheap, unskilled labour to be used for the white man's benefit.

I take the opposite view. From the moment Van Riebeeck and his men first clapped eyes on the Khoikhoi, there entered into the reckoning the notion that non-whites were inferior and not really human beings at all. If this is thought fanciful then one may look at what the Turks did to the Armenians in 1915, or, the gaudiest example of all, what the Nazis did to the Jews. In Germany the holocaust was only possible because the victims were not regarded as human, but as *untermensche*, no better than animals. I do not mean to suggest that the Afrikaners in South Africa have ever entertained the idea of gas ovens or extermination camps. On the contrary they are, paradoxically, too moral for that. Whatever measures they have taken against blacks have always in one way or another been justified either by quasi-scientific evidence, biblical witness or historical precedent. Nevertheless all their actions are motivated by the conviction, deeply rooted and arcane, that the non-whites are non-persons, uncivilised, barbaric, of limited intelligence. If South Africa had been a country poor in natural resources, the same standards would have been imposed. Economic advantage, I suggest, was born of misinformed concepts of racial superiority. But whichever theory is acceptable, the same question has to be asked: in the prevailing circumstances what was the black man to do?

Two years after the Act of Union, on 8 January 1912, an event took place that was to be of great political importance for the future. Unnoticed by the white rulers or, perhaps, just ignored, the South African Native National Congress came into being. Some years later it was to change its name to the African National Congress, the ANC. Ironically, this event preceded by only two years the formation of the National Party, which spoke for Afrikanerdom. Although previous attempts in the late nineteenth century and again in 1908 to represent black interests had failed, the time seemed right to try again.

The ANC's guiding lights were Pixley ka Izaka Seme and the Reverend John Dube from Natal. Seme was a lawyer with a splendid academic background: Columbia University, Oxford and the Inns of Court. And it should be remembered that any black capable of such achievement must have been quite outstanding, for the educational dice were heavily loaded against him. 'We must think in wider political terms', he declared, 'for we are one people.' His immediate goal was to unite the disparate black communities, diagnosing tribal divisions as the cause of much misery. His chief aims, however, were to fight racial discrimination and achieve civil rights for all.

He called a conference and from all over southern Africa there came together blacks of different tribes and backgrounds, speaking a variety of languages. Dube, who was elected President, articulated what their strategy was to be. The government of the day would be approached 'not with *assegais* but respectfully as loyal subjects, with the intention of airing their grievances and removing the obstacles of poverty, prejudice and discriminatory legislation'. The ANC's tactics were to be legal and conciliatory, favouring petitions and deputations: in no sense were they anti-white. From the beginning the ANC denounced racism.

Seme became Treasurer, and a journalist, Solomon Tshekisho Plaatje, was the first Secretary-General. Sol T. Plaatje (pronounced 'ply-key') was, incidentally, an extraordinary figure: during the Boer War, in 1899, he acted as interpreter to the Mafeking court while the town was under siege. He kept a journal of daily life which was only discovered 71 years later and is an important piece of Africana. Self-educated, he became a newspaper editor, a public speaker and the author of a novel called *Mhudi*, which is thought to be one of the first written by a black South African.

This inaugural conference in Bloemfontein was organised in an original and interesting way. The model was the American Congress, but there were also features of the British parliamentary system such as a Speaker and an Upper House of Chiefs. At the opening of the meeting a hymn was sung. Composed by a Xhosa, Enoch Sontonga, it was called 'Nkosi Sikilel' iAfrika' – 'Lord Bless Africa' – and became the anthem of the ANC. The congress was dignified and solemn, as if the delegates were determined to show themselves as responsible, capable men which, indeed, they were. But both the substance and form of their deliberations went unheeded.

In the years of Nelson Mandela's childhood and adolescence, the ANC pursued its policy of non-violent protest which was, predictably, answered violently. By the time Mandela was twelve, in 1930, Congress had degenerated into a debating society in which high-minded resolutions were passed but never acted on. Its only lasting contribution from this period was to adopt, in 1925, a flag of black, green and gold to symbolise the people, the land and resources.

Mandela was sent to a mission school where he would have learned the basic skills and received the customary indoctrination which was also meted out to white children but with perhaps less harmful effects. Because history is usually written by the victors, Mandela would have learned of the Kaffir Wars, of how 'natives' (the other euphemism then for blacks) were savages and cattle thieves, of how a small group of brave Boers with guns defended themselves against the barbaric Kaffir hordes armed with spears and shields. At home, however, the balance would undoubtedly have been redressed. The villains of the white history books were the heroes of the black fireside. But as well as the epic tales of heroism, he would certainly have heard the saddest of all Xhosa tales, that of *Nongqause*, the story of a national suicide. It is worth recording here for it is a cautionary tale, containing a moral which concerns the aspirations and the collective will of a once great people.

In the Eastern Cape, during the first months of 1856, rumours of war between settlers and Xhosa were rife. The Xhosa had been driven from their homes and, it was reported, had lost the will to fight. Neverthless, the rumours persisted. In one of the lesser Xhosa chiefdoms, along the banks of the Gxara River, there was a small village of some twenty or thirty huts. In one of these huts lived a young girl of thirteen or fourteen, Nongquase. Her only distinction was that her uncle, the brother of her dead father, was Mhlakaza, a renowned Xhosa seer. Early one morning in May she went down to the river to bathe and fetch water and there she saw cattle grazing, guarded by men she did not recognise. She was certain they had not been there when she first entered the water. They made no noise: the cattle trod silently and when the men talked she was unable to hear their voices. One of the men raised his hand in greeting and Nongquase became convinced that this was her dead father whom she had never known. Then the men disappeared and Nongquase saw, or thought she saw, the horns of the oxen among the rushes, as though the cattle were being driven deep into the river. She ran back to the village and reported what she had seen to her mysterious uncle, Mhlakaza.

Alone, Mhlakaza went down to the river to see for himself. When he returned he confirmed Nongquase's story to the chief's council, the *ilizwe*: he, too, had seen these strangers and, indeed, one of them he recognised as his dead brother. Mhlakaza was told to go back to the village and purify himself before returning. After performing the necessary rites, he ventured once more to the banks of the river and returned with a cryptic message. 'I saw my brother again', he said, 'and other warriors. I was told many things. Great sacrifices are demanded of us.' When he was asked who these other soldiers were, he replied, 'They are Russians, black like ourselves. And they have come to drive the English back into the sea.' (At the time the British were fighting in the Crimea.) What exactly Mhlakaza was told by the shades was for the chief's ear alone, but presently messengers were sent to the royal *kraal* of the Paramount Chief, Kreli, and the message was made public. The Xhosa, the shades had said, must kill all their cattle and plant no crops and only then would the white man be driven into the sea. And on that great day, it was promised, herds of cattle would rise from the ground and the dead ancestors of the Xhosa would also rise. The crops would grow before their eyes. Later, the prophesy was embellished. Nongquase had further visitations from the shades, who told her that the great day would be preceded by a terrible whirlwind and the whites would be turned into frogs, mice and ants. Chief Kreli ordered his people to do what the shades commanded.

Estimates put the number of cattle slaughtered at 200,000. Some white observers said that the Xhosa were driven by blind superstition, which only went to show how primitive and barbaric they really were. Later, another theory was offered: the slaughter was part of a highly-orchestrated action which was intended to stir the people into a frenzy in order that they might rediscover the will to destroy their enemies. By the end of 1856, the Xhosa were starving on a massive scale and dying in their thousands. White men of good will did their best to avert the disaster but to no avail. Mhlakaza announced that 18 February 1857 would be the day of the resurrection. Two blood-red suns would rise, he said, but then changed his mind. Only one sun would rise but it would move around the sky and re-set in the east.

The day dawned and the sun rose as usual. Neither ancestors nor cattle appeared, and the crops did not suddenly grow. Desparate, the Xhosa poured into the colony in search of food. Thousands died. The Xhosa had suffered a devastating blow, their traditional homelands depopulated. Mhlakaza himself died of hunger but Nongquase survived and lived to an old age. Often she was questioned about the event in which she had played a key role. Was she ordered to do what she did? Or had she been overcome by her imagination? Perhaps she had really seen men and cattle in the river? She refused to answer and remained silent on the subject until her death.

Despair, then, was also one of Nelson Mandela's legacies from the past.

2

THE ARTICLED CLERK

In 1930, when Mandela was twelve, his father, Chief Henry, was taken seriously ill. The dying man was anxious about his son's future, for he must have perceived in Mandela gifts that were both rare and valuable. The boy was obviously intelligent and a conscientious student, but there was something in his character more difficult to define and pin down: even in adolescence, it seems, Mandela evinced qualities of leadership; his personality drew others to him. Wanting to do the best for his son, Chief Henry asked the acting Paramount Chief, David Dalindyebo, to become guardian to the boy and to see that he was properly educated. Dalindyebo agreed.

Dictatorial, loving, proud, Dalindyebo took this new responsibility seriously and brought his ward to live with him at the Chief's Great Place, Mqekezweni. Here politics were discussed and Mandela thrived on the stories of the past, the difficulties of the present, the plans for the future. 'The Elders would tell us about the liberation', he wrote,

and how it was fought by our ancestors in defence of our country, as well as the acts of valour performed by generals and soldiers during those epic days. I hoped, and vowed then, that amongst the pleasures that life might offer me, would be the opportunity to serve my people and make my own contribution to their struggle for freedom.

At the age of sixteen Mandela underwent the Xhosa initiation to manhood which includes the rite of circumcision, the *Ukwalusa*, and is the most important event in any male's life. Until that time a boy among the Xhosa is a 'thing' and not a person. Only after his term in the initiation school is he regarded as a man. The full ritual is spread over a period of about three months and comprises the 'going in' which involves the actual circumcision, and the 'coming out' which occurs at the end of a period of isolation. So, probably in March 1934, Mandela entered the initiation school on the banks of the Mbashe River, the place where many of his ancestors had been circumcised, and had his 'coming out' around May. 'By the standards of my tribe', he wrote, 'I was now a man ready to take part in the "parliament" of the tribe Imbizo.'

The man, however, was still a student attending Clarkebury, a nearby training college. He looked forward to the holidays when he was able to witness the Paramount Chief presiding over his court to which minor chiefs brought their grievances. Mandela would listen wrapt to the cases for the prosecution and defence, the cross-examination of witnesses, all the while trying to predict the final judgement by Dalindyebo and his councillors. This was the beginning of his ambition to become a lawyer. In due course he was sent to Healdtown, a Methodist high school where he matriculated, and afterwards to Fort Hare College, in the village of Alice in the Eastern Cape, to study for a Bachelor of Arts degree. But racial politics erupted in the college and as a result Mandela's life was temporarily disrupted.

Fort Hare was the equivalent of a university college. In 1905 the Inter-Colonial Native Affairs Commission recommended 'that a central Native College or similar institution be established and aided by the various states, for training Native teachers, and in order to afford opportunities for higher education to Native students'. However, the scheme did not come to fruition until after the founding of the Union. In 1914 the draft constitution of such a college was finally adopted and it was established as the South African Native College at Fort Hare in the Victoria East district, Cape Province. Making steady progress, the college was eventually able to provide a liberal education of university standard and was affiliated to Rhodes University, Grahamstown. By the time Mandela was an undergraduate, Fort Hare had become a centre of excellence and therefore, in the eyes of the white authorities, a dangerous place.

At Fort Hare, Mandela made one of the most important friendships of his life, for it was here he first met Oliver Tambo. One year Mandela's senior, Tambo, the son of a peasant farmer, was also from the Transkei. He was academically outstanding and attended St Peter's, Johannesburg, which had the curious distinction of being called the African Eton. In 1938 he took a first-class matriculation and was awarded a scholarship to Fort Hare where he studied for a degree in science. Years later he would write that Mandela was

> ... passionate, emotional, sensitive, quickly stung to bitterness and retaliation by insult and patronage. He has a natural air of

authority. He cannot help magnetizing a crowd: he is commanding with a tall, handsome bearing ...

These attributes were already pronounced at Fort Hare, for when the authorities reduced the powers of the Students' Representative Council of which Mandela was a member, he was outraged and immediately joined a protest boycott. The college issued an ultimatum that the students must abandon the boycott or face the consequences. Mandela continued the boycott. This was his first political act of any consequence and it resulted in his suspension from the college and the temporary interruption of his friendship with Tambo. Unrepentant, Mandela returned to Mqekezweni and to the wrath of the Paramount Chief. Dalindyebo ordered him to accept the college's terms of surrender so that he could resume his studies, but Mandela was saved from defying his guardian by an unexpected turn of events. 'My guardian', Mandela remembered

... felt it was time for me to get married. He loved me very much and looked after me as diligently as my father had, but he was no democrat and did not think it worthwhile to consult me about a wife. He selected a girl, fat and dignified, paid lobola and arrangements were afoot for the wedding. I escaped to Johannesburg.

He was about to embark on the most fateful journey of his young life. From the comparative peace of the countryside, he was to thrust himself into the heart of white supremacy maintained by a repressive political system.

When Mandela came to Johannesburg in 1941, the Union of South Africa was at war with Nazi Germany. The declaration had been made on 6 September 1939 after a political crisis which resulted in the resignation of the Prime Minister, General James Barry Munnik Hertzog. As founder and leader of the National Party, which represented the Afrikaners, Hertzog had predictably opposed South Africa's participation on the side of the British. He was defeated in the House of Assembly by 80 votes to 67, the majority of those against him being mostly English-speaking. Immediately Hertzog went to the Governor-General, Sir Patrick Duncan, asked him to dissolve Parliament and to put the issue to a general election. Duncan refused and instead invited Herzog's coalition colleague, General Jan

Christian Smuts, to form a new ministry. It was the climax of a conflict within the Boer community which had been festering for more than twenty years.

That conflict holds the key to South Africa's future misery. Since whites were the rulers, we may unfortunately take it for granted that legislation, in so far as it affected land, property, work, education, freedom of movement and voting rights, was always loaded heavily against non-whites. The government of any day was intent on securing a cheap labour force confined to certain districts, controlled in its mobility and without a say in its affairs. Successive Acts of Parliament dealing with these problems were racist, cruel, brutal and morally indefensible. Two examples will suffice: under the infamous Natives Land Act of 1913, eight million Africans were allowed 12.7 per cent of the land; the two million whites were free to develop 87 per cent. In 1923 the hateful Pass Laws were codified. An African needed a pass for work, travel, and to be out after curfew at night. If he could not produce the document he was subject to a fine or, more often, imprisonment. The whites, whatever their language or allegiance, supported and encouraged such measures. What became known colloquially as the 'Colour Bar' was, by consensus, in-stitutionalised and legalised. Within the Boer community, however, other influences were at work, inspired by a need for a collective identity and cultural allegiance. These instincts were not motives in themselves. The real stimulus was the bitterness of defeat in war and of ancient hatreds. When the Boers at last found their sense of *volk*, they proved to be an unstoppable force – and it was that force with which Mandela and his colleagues had eventually to contend.

The virus that invaded the Boer mentality was nationalism. The Boers, with some English support, had formed the first South African government in 1910. The South African Party was led for the most part by distinguished Boer War leaders. The first Prime Minister was General Louis Botha and he included in his Cabinet two other generals, Hertzog and Smuts. Their first priority was to deal with the process of urbanisation, which was taking place at an alarming rate and causing enormous hardship. The traditional rural white economy was in shreds, destroyed by modernisation. Whites, mostly Afrikaners, were being displaced from the countryside by the advance of the railways, a law of inheritance which subdivided property, and a general movement towards the cities where the development of the mines and industries held out the promise of well-paid work. The 'poor whites', as they were called, flooded into the towns and found themselves in direct competition with blacks who were in a similar, though much worse, plight. So desperate was the displaced black rural community that 'squatting' on white farms was commonplace and further aggravated the tensions between races. When action had to be taken, it did not require a prophet to foretell which section of the community the government would favour.

But not all Boers were united behind Botha and Smuts. The stumbling-block was, as ever, their attitude to London, and to the English-speaking members of the white South African community. Neither leader wanted to alienate Britain and went to great lengths to placate and assist big business, which was then dominated by English-speakers. To the Boers it seemed that their own government was pursuing an unnecessarily pro-British policy. Smuts came in for most criticism. He had been a member of Lloyd George's Imperial War Cabinet and was accused, with justification, of being an anglophile and an imperialist. He managed to alienate not only the poorer Boers but also the intelligentsia within his own party; in so doing he made possible a coalition of the two which was to have dire consequences for South Africa. Afrikaner nationalism took hold. Although Dutch was officially their main language, the intellectuals seized on Afrikaans and waved it about like a cultural flag. Their aim was to make it an acceptable tongue, to elevate it from the kitchen in which it was mostly spoken. The political leader of the *volk* was Barry Hertzog. True, he did not believe that Afrikaner nationalism meant Afrikaner supremacy, but that was naive of him. Campaigning within the Cabinet for equality of the Dutch and English languages, he also questioned certain residual rights in foreign policy which the British had retained. For example, he asked, if Britain went to war, was South Africa automatically obliged to fight as its ally? His attitude alienated him from Botha and Smuts. At the beginning of 1914 he founded the National Party, an offshoot of which in time would come to rule South Africa with an iron hand and be responsible for the appalling plight the country finds itself in the last decades of the present century.

In 1922 the mine-owners made it known that they were preparing to employ blacks in semi-skilled work. The threat to white workers was obvious and the white mine-workers' union called out its members on strike. Smuts, who had succeeded Botha as Prime Minister in 1919, used the white army to crush a white strike which was in danger of escalating into a small-scale rebellion. This draconian measure was seen by the Boers as further proof of Smuts's perfidy. He would never again have the full confidence of his own people.

To bolster Hertzog's policy that Afrikaners and English-speakers should work side by side, the English-led Labour Party, whose constituency was white workers, joined forces with him and in the election of 1924 the coalition unseated Smuts. Astonishingly, Hertzog won the support of Coloureds in the Cape and even of some black organisations who were, it seems, willing to give the Afrikaners a chance or, at least, the benefit of the doubt. Herzog made Afrikaans an official language, gave the Union its flag, and protected home industries. In imperial conferences he helped pave the way for the Statute of Westminster in 1931, by which Britain recognised the equality of the dominions, including their right to secede. But by then external forces were beginning to have an effect on South African politics. The crisis of capitalism, the Depression, produced even worse poverty among whites, so much so that a fifth of the white population was living below the bread-line. The spectre of the 'poor white' became fixed in the Afrikaner mind. In 1933 Hertzog was forced into a new coalition, this time with Smuts's South African Party; the following year they merged as the United Party. Together, with Afrikaner support, they carried through a tough racial policy of greater segregation, disenfranchisement of Cape blacks and the expansion of the Native Reserves. However, not all Afrikaners felt able to support the 'fusion', as the merger of the two parties was known; many decided the government's policies were not tough enough, either in regard to nationalism or racism. The leader of the dissatisfaction was a former Minister of the Interior, Education and Public Health, Dr Daniel François Malan. He broke away and formed a new party: the Purified National Party, dedicated to full republicanism and Afrikaner supremacy. This pattern of breakaway groups, each time more and more extreme, continues to this day and haunts the leaders of the mainstream. Michael Attwell summed up the process in his book *South Africa: Background to the Crisis*:

> Throughout Afrikaner history, leaders have been produced who canalize and articulate Afrikaner nationalism. When they appear to sacrifice Afrikaner hegemony in the interests of broader co-operation, they are jettisoned and new leaders emerge to continue the fight for supremacy.

Beneath the surface, the Purified National Party was being fed by a sinister, poisoned stream. A secret organisation, the *Broederbond*, the Band of Brothers, a sort of nationalist masonic lodge, had come into being. With front organisations promoting Afrikaans language, culture and identity, its more profound purpose was to ensure that Afrikaners were placed in key positions of power and influence. The Chairman in 1932, Professor J. C. van Rooy of Potchefstroom University, made this intent clear if not public. In a secret message to members, he wrote:

> After the cultural and economic needs, the Afrikaner Broederbond will have to devote its attention to the political needs of our people. And here the aim must be a completely independent, genuine Afrikaans government for South Africa. A government which, by its embodiment of our own personal Head of State, bone of our bone and flesh of our flesh, will inspire us and bind us together in irresistible unity and strength.

To the *Broederbond* belonged all future National Party Prime Ministers. At its meetings, Dr Hendrik Verwoerd, a social psychologist at Stellenbosch University, first articulated his intractable philosophy, which in time was to earn him the soubriquet, 'Apostle of Apartheid'; and from its ranks, in defiance of the national mood to fight against Hitler, was born the even more secret *Ossewabrandwag* (Ox-wagon Sentinel), fascist and pro-Nazi. One of its members, who was interned for his activities was also to be a future Prime Minister: John Vorster.

Despite the fact that great numbers of their fellow-countrymen were fighting against Fascism, to the hard-line Afrikaners the Second World War was an irritating diversion from their main objective. This period is of interest to us here only because Mandela, during those years, escaped the discipline of his guardian and arrived in Johannesburg, one young black among thousands who converged on the city in search of work. With so many men at the front – 'up North' – there was a constant demand for labour.

Mandela, in the company of a nephew, had travelled by bus and train from the Eastern Cape, through Natal and into the highveld of the Transvaal. They would have had to sit in an overcrowded third-class carriage – 'Non-Europeans Only' – and sleep sitting up. The end of the journey was signalled by the sight of mine dumps, gold-tipped, like defunct volcanoes: Egoli, City of Gold, Johannesburg. Mandela's bewilderment must have been immense. Here he was, a product of the quiet countryside, of what may be described as a privileged background, aristocratic, educated, proud.

And what did he encounter? A modern city, New York in miniature, skyscrapers, traffic, noise, bustle. Everywhere he would have seen the *Slegs vir Blankes* – Europeans Only – signs and had his first true experience of the Colour Bar. But the real and more profound humiliation was yet to come. In order to find somewhere to live, he set out for a 'Native location', Alexandra, to the northeast of the city. This was, in Oliver Tambo's words, Mandela's first encounter 'with the lot of the urban African in a teeming African township: overcrowding, incessant raids for passes, arrests, poverty, the pin-pricks and frustrations of White rule'.

He had also to find work, and so he and his nephew applied for a job at Crown Mines. Mandela, by a splendid irony, was employed as a policeman with the assurance that, should a vacancy occur, he would become a clerk. His job was to guard the gate to the compound in which the black miners were housed. He was given an ill-fitting uniform, a whistle and a weapon called a *knobkerrie* which is a short thick stick with a knobbled head. It is worth recording that his nephew, who was taken on as a trainee clerk, ended up Chief Justice Mtirara of the Transkeian Territorial Authority. Mandela's contribution to law and order was unremarkable and brief. In a matter of days an emissary of the Paramount Chief had discovered his whereabouts; Mandela took to his heels and sought anonymity in Alexandra Township.

The two men who could relate exactly what happened next are unfortunately not available to questions from historians. But either through an acquaintance or because one sought out the other, Mandela came into contact with Walter Max Ulyate Sisulu. It was a fateful meeting. Sisulu was what would be called today 'street-wise': he knew his way around the townships, kept his ear to the ground and was always on the look-out for likely young men who shared his political interests. Six years older than Mandela, Sisulu also hailed from the Transkei, but his experience of life, by contrast, was varied and harsh: he had worked as a miner underground, and as a 'kitchen-boy' in a white household; he had been employed in factories but inevitably fallen foul of the white bosses. He had also been imprisoned: one evening after work, returning to the township by train, he saw a white ticket inspector unfairly confiscate an African child's season ticket. He asked the official to explain the action. The man struck him and Sisulu hit back. He was arrested and, for the first time, imprisoned. Going from job to job, he still found the hours

Previous page;
Mandela in
national dress

Mandela as
a young man

The young lawyer in
the Mandela and
Tambo law office in
Johannesburg, 1952

National volunteer-in-chief. During the 1952 defiance campaign,
Mandela travelled the country enlisting volunteers to defy the apartheid laws.
A scene from the film

A scene from the film: Mandela as national volunteer-in-chief

Swanepoel serves
banning orders on
Mandela, Sisulu and
Tambo in 1952:
a scene from the film

The treason trial,
1956-60: a scene
from the film

Mandela during a recess in the treason trial, 1956-60

Previously unpublished photographs showing Nelson Mandela burning his pass book, circa 1956

and energy to study for his Junior Certificate by correspondence. He was helped in this by his mother, with whom he lived, and who supported them both by taking in washing for white families. At the time of his meeting with Mandela, Sisulu was dealing in real estate on a pitifully small scale, trying to secure for blacks what little freehold land was available to them. He offered Mandela a job as an estate agent at £2 per month plus commission. 'It was', Mandela later recalled, 'the most difficult time in my life.'

Employee and employer became fast friends. Mandela confided his ambition to become a lawyer and Sisulu made it financially possible for the first step to be taken: Mandela would study for a Bachelor of Arts degree by correspondence course. When the time came for the graduation ceremony, Sisulu lent him money for a new suit, and there is no doubt Mandela would have gone to great trouble in his choice: smart, well-fitting clothes were always one of his conceits. And it was Sisulu who introduced Mandela to a firm of white lawyers, Witkin, Sidelsky and Eidelman, to whom he was articled in 1942 while studying law part time at the University of the Witwatersrand.

Apart from his contacts with officials and teachers in the Transkei, this was Mandela's first close encounter with Europeans. And since the law firm took in young promising blacks, its general attitude was more liberal than most. Even so, the Colour Bar was never far beneath the surface. Mandela recalled two particular incidents:

On my first day at the office the White senior typist said, 'Look, Nelson, we have no colour bar here. When the tea-boy brings the tea come and get yours from the tray. We have brought two new cups for you and Gaur Radike – another African employee. You must use them. Tell Gaur about your cups. Be careful of him, Nelson, he is a bad influence.' I duly told Gaur whose response was, 'I will show you. Do exactly as I do.' When the tea arrived Gaur boycotted the new cups and picked one of the old ones. I had no desire to quarrel with him or the senior typist, so for months I did not drink tea.

Some months later a new typist, also White, was in the habit of asking me for work when she had nothing to do. One day I was dictating to her when a White client came in. She was obviously embarrassed and, to demonstrate that I was not her employer, she took 6d. from her purse and said, 'Mandela, please go and get me some hair shampoo from the chemist.'

These were mild examples of white attitudes. From the way he writes about them, one can detect his amusement and a certain disdain that was not arrogance but the confidence which came from knowing his own worth. He was less concerned with taking offence than with the work in hand, which was proving more and more demanding: added to his part-time studies at the university, he had long train journeys to and from lectures, to and from the law office, and the eleven p.m. curfew to obey. Even so, he found time to attend a township gymnasium where he trained hard. Physical fitness, he discovered, went hand in hand with intellectual effort, and he became a competent boxer.

He liked the company of women and they were attracted to him. Tall, well-built, always immaculately dressed, he cut a dashing figure. While still a student he met and married Evelyn Ntoko Mase, a nurse at the City Deep Mine Hospital. Having a regular job she was able to help with his fees. By then Sisulu had also married a nurse, Albertina, and the couples lived near each other in Orlando, an ugly, barren, sprawling township to the southwest of Johannesburg, an area now called Soweto – a name crudely derived from *southwe*stern *to*wnships.

These were exciting days for the young articled clerk and they bear witness to his prodigious energies, which thrived on activity and movement. His enormous vitality was fed by all the interweaving strands which were never separate or compartmentalised. Whatever Mandela undertook he regarded simply as one process, as his way of being. And it was now that he began to entertain another passion that would, increasingly, take up more and more of his time and, eventually, give focus and meaning to his life.

The African National Congress had, as we have seen, lost much of its early impetus in the 1930s. But by the outbreak of war and in response to Hertzog's Segregation Bills, it was again beginning to flex its muscles. This was largely due to an Anglican minister, James Calata, who had become Secretary-General. Although extremely poor and chronically ill, he was persistent and persuasive. To his good fortune his own appointment coincided with the election, in December 1940, of a new and energetic President-General, Dr A. B. Xuma, who had a large medical practice in Johannesburg. It was after hearing one of Xuma's speeches that Walter Sisulu was inspired to join the ANC. Other intellectuals began to play a part, notably Professor Z. K. Matthews, social anthropologist and expert in native law and administration at Fort Hare. Matthews had a certain reputation in educational circles abroad and he was to play an important role in the ANC's revival.

The mood of township blacks lurched between despair and anger. With wages usually below subsistence level, the black trades union asked to meet employers in order to negotiate for better conditions. When their requests were refused, they called their members out on strike. Smuts answered with War Measure 145, which made all such industrial action illegal. But it was a difficult law to enforce, and strikes of one kind or another continued. In Alexandra, when the bus fares were increased, people walked to and from work in the bitter cold. It took nine days for the bus company to surrender. When a fare increase was tried again in 1944, the people walked for seven weeks to achieve victory.

To answer the seemingly unending measures of repression, the new ANC leadership did not adopt the organisation's traditional stance of trying merely to ameliorate the blacks' condition; instead, in a document entitled *African Claims*, Xuma and Matthews advocated, among other things, full citizenship rights including the vote. They also struck a chord of African nationalism, a sense of brotherhood with all black people of Africa under colonial rule. These aims may have indicated a shift in policy, but the methods of achieving them still smacked of a longing to be accepted by the white ruling class. Dr Xuma believed in delegations to meet the government, but these were either rebuffed or insulted. He came to be regarded as too moderate. Within the ranks of the ANC an undercurrent of discontent was bubbling. The leaders of this rebellion, who later came to be called the 'young Turks', were intellectual and radical. They included Walter Sisulu, Nelson Mandela and his friend from Fort Hare days, Oliver Tambo.

Mandela and Tambo had renewed their friendship in 1944 when Tambo came to St Peter's School in Johannesburg to teach science and mathematics; soon both men found themselves in the thick of African politics. 'We were never really young', Tambo said. 'There were no dances, hardly a cinema, but meetings, discussions, every night, every weekend.' The leader of these young Turks was a Zulu, Anton Muziwakhe Lembede, the son of poor farm labourers who had somehow managed to find the money for his primary education. By all accounts he had a magnetic personality and was intellectually brilliant. First a teacher, then a lawyer, Lembede was the driving force behind the able young professionals who now formed themselves into a Youth League. Among its founding members were the lawyer, A. P. Mda, Robert Sobukwe, a university lecturer, and Govan Mbeki. They met in Sisulu's office and formulated their aim to 'galvanise' the ANC which, while acknowledging its historical and symbolic importance, they saw as organisationally flawed, and as 'regarding itself as a body of gentlemen with clean hands'. The Youth League, with Lembede as President and Tambo as Secretary, was to provide the ANC with a new and more aggressive philosophy.

In March 1944 they published a manifesto originally drafted by Mda and worked on by Mandela and others. The preamble clearly proclaims the League's belief in Africanism, which did not mean black racialism. What the Youth Leaguers wanted was full democracy in South Africa which, of course, meant majority rule. The note they sounded was for African nationalism, their motto, 'AFRICA'S CAUSE MUST TRIUMPH'. Their creed included the belief that African liberation of Africans must be achieved by Africans themselves. While they rejected foreign leadership, they nevertheless acknowledged the value of borrowing what was useful from foreign ideologies. They formulated policies on land reform, trades unions and education. It is an important document, for in many ways it was to set the tone for the future.

Most of the members of the Youth League, and especially Mandela, were deeply anti-communist. Mary Benson, in her book, *Nelson Mandela*, has this to say:

... when Ruth First, as Secretary of the Progressive Youth Council [a Communist Party organisation] approached them, inviting their affiliation, their reply was a firm refusal.

Bram Fischer, an Afrikaner who was a communist and who, as an advocate, had assisted Xuma in drawing up a more democratic constitution for the ANC, found Mandela and Sisulu – 'young Turks' as he called them – not only anti-communist but against cooperation with whites ...

The Youth League believed that such cooperation would undermine their struggle; besides, white communists regarded their nationalism as 'chauvinistic'. Furthermore, communist emphasis on division between working class and capitalists clouded the main issue of uniting all Africans. Lembede, Mandela, Sisulu and Tambo tried to force African communists to resign from the Party if they were to remain in the ANC and introduced a motion to this effect at an annual conference.

With the end of the war, optimism in all sections of South African society ran high. The ANC marched in the victory parade in Johannesburg, and its members may be forgiven for believing that the country's white leaders were prepared to build a new society. After all, Smuts had helped to draft the preamble to the Charter of the United Nations which included these sentiments:

> To reaffirm faith in fundamental human rights, in the dignity and worth of the human person, in the equal rights of men and women and of nations large and small ...
>
> To promote social progress and better standards of life ...
>
> To practice tolerance and live together in peace with one another as good neighbours ...

Did he mean to include South Africa? Apparently not. Barely a year after the end of the war, Smuts introduced a 'Ghetto' Bill aimed at confining the Indian community to certain areas. But then Smuts saw himself as others saw him: a great world statesman who had been declared by Oxford University to be 'the strength and stay of the Commonwealth'. He had been appointed a British Field-Marshal, elected Chancellor of Cambridge University, was a friend of Winston Churchill, a confidant of King George VI and was shortly to receive the highly-prized Order of Merit. The running of South Africa he left largely to his deputy, J. H. Hofmeyr. The country would pay dearly for his personal ambition and negligence.

In February 1947 King George VI, Queen Elizabeth and their daughters, the Princesses Elizabeth and Margaret Rose, arrived in Cape Town to begin a tour of the country. The Transvaal Nationalist daily, *Die Transvaler*, under its editor Dr Verwoerd, totally ignored the event. Smuts, however, was in his element: he was himself a great royalist and believed the visit would somehow boost his chances in a general election which he was obliged to call in the near future. A year later, on 8 March 1948, Smuts announced to the House of Assembly that the election would be held in late May or early June. When Parliament rose Smuts appeared to be in an invulnerable position. In a house of 153 seats, his United Party held 89. The main opposition party, the Nationalists led by Dr Malan, held forty-nine, other parties twelve, and three seats were held by the Natives' Representatives. Smuts, therefore, had an absolute majority.

The central issue of the campaign was the future of white South Africa, of which Malan had made himself the champion. In the

United Party the main burden of the debate fell upon Smuts's deputy and heir-apparent, the Cape liberal, J. H. Hofmeyr. Malan was proposing separation of the races and a new word became current to describe that policy: apartheid. According to his biographer, Alan Paton, Hofmeyr repeated a statement he had made in 1936: if racial separation of black and white could be complete, he would say a great deal in favour of it. Separation, he continued, had become a magic word, and had put ministers of religion and professors under its spell, but they did not understand that it was impossible. Hofmeyr favoured the policy of trusteeship, which was a euphemism for paternalism.

> 'I am not in favour of a policy of assimilation. I have repeatedly stated that the essential difference between Europeans and non-Europeans must be taken into consideration. The policy of Christian trusteeship I have in mind does not mean suppression, nor does it mean equality. It means the realisation of our responsibility not to ignore the interests of people of whom we are the guardians.'

Not surprisingly, trusteeship had been bitterly attacked in the Youth League's manifesto. Nevertheless, it meant the slowing down of segregation. Hofmeyr had attempted to improve welfare payments to blacks and he had instigated a go-slow on enforcing the Pass Laws. Small concessions but, given the realities of white South African politics, the United Party certainly represented the lesser of two evils.

The Nationalists directed the main force of their attack against him, as though Smuts had already become irrelevant. A pamphlet declared that the road Hofmeyr was following 'leads to equality, and the downfall of white South Africa!' They wanted *baasskap*, white supremacy; Hofmeyr offered *leierskap*, leadership, of which he said, 'We must not dominate, we must lead, I do not doubt that the European will always maintain the leadership on merit.' To which a leading Nationalist and future Prime Minister, J. G. Strijdom, replied, 'I never knew that such stupidity could come from such a clever mind – either it is stupidity or political deception.' Hofmeyr was painted as an extremist. The United Party responded lamely by trying to prove that he was not as bad, nor as extreme, as he was painted. In desperation, they turned their guns on Dr Malan's past, on his anti-Semitism and pro-Nazi views. The voters were not concerned with Dr Malan's past; it was his uncompromising present which attracted them.

To Mandela and his friends the election of 1948 was, like Smuts, irrelevant. They had no vote and no way of influencing the niceties of the white political debate. Whichever party won, they saw little hope for their people: *leierskap* or *baasskap*, trusteeship or apartheid, the lot of the non-whites would, they knew, be in much the same position as before. The election took place on 26 May 1948. By the following evening it was clear that Smuts would not command an absolute majority in the House; by the following morning it was clear he would have no majority at all. Smuts himself was defeated in his own constituency by 244 votes. Apartheid was about to become a reality, but just what that meant in terms of repression, violence, cruelty and suffering was not yet wholly apparent. However, Mandela must have realised that the struggle against white supremacy was bound to enter a new phase. When he had qualified as a lawyer one of the partners in the firm to which he had been articled gave Mandela some advice. Mr Sidelsky, a Polish Jew, to whom Mandela said he would always be indebted for his kindness and encouragement, begged Mandela to concentrate on becoming a good lawyer. Perhaps he offered the example of the Jews who believed that excellence in a chosen profession earned the respect of all sections of the community and thus diminished racism. Whatever Mandela did in the future, Sidelsky said, he should at all costs avoid politics. It was advice Mandela was unable to accept.

PART TWO

THE MAN
AND THE STRUGGLE

FROM THE SCREENPLAY

FADE IN:
EXT. SHANTYTOWN STREET (ALEXANDRA TOWNSHIP). DAY.
Matchbox houses, cardboard roofs. Few people about. One or two sit and chatter in the sun; others walking or going about their daily business. Peaceful, calm.
SUPERIMPOSE:

1948

Feed in the SOUND of the House of Assembly: a murmur becoming noisy, excited; then:

ASSEMBLY SPEAKER'S VOICE
Order, order!
(*Noise subsides*)
The Prime Minister, Dr Malan.

Cheers.

PRIME MINISTER'S VOICE
Mr Speaker, today South Africa belongs
to us.

Cheers.

Into the shantytown street screech two police vans and out of them pour POLICEMEN who begin a round-up for Passes. They haul people to their feet, search them, shout at them, bully them, beat them and all the time shouting 'Pass! Pass! Pass!'

During this:

PRIME MINISTER'S VOICE
(*continuing*)
We shall be introducing legislation to
implement our policy which we call
Apartheid, the separation between the
races.

THE POLICE drag drinkers out of a shebeen (an illegal drinking hall) and start bundling them into a van. A woman tries to run away. A POLICEMAN chases her and beats her.

During this:

> PRIME MINISTER'S VOICE
> (*continuing*)
> Races will live and travel separately.
> Education will be separate for all
> groups at all levels. Native reserves
> will become black homelands. Work
> fitting for the white man will be
> reserved for him and him alone.

And as the white POLICE *drag the black woman into the van*

CUT TO:

EXT. ANOTHER SHANTYTOWN STREET. DAY.
> *Tin shacks, corrugated tin roofs. Empty. Silent. Suddenly an enormous* BULLDOZER *lumbers into shot and starts to demolish the camp. Black* WOMEN *and* CHILDREN *watch helplessly under the eyes of smiling white* POLICEMEN. *The dreadful noise of grating metal on metal.*

> PRIME MINISTER'S VOICE
> (*continuing*)
> Apartheid rests on three unarguable
> foundations: Afrikaner experience, our
> experience, scientific proof that the
> white man is a superior being, and
> biblical witness. Apartheid represents
> Divine Will.

And as the bulldozer comes menacingly towards CAMERA

CUT TO:

EXT. COUNTRYSIDE. DAY.
> *A* TRAIN *snaking through the African countryside.*
> SUPERIMPOSE TITLE, MAIN CREDITS *and*
> ### 1952

EXT. SMALL COUNTRY SIDING. DAY.
> TRAIN *comes to a halt. One man gets off, carrying a suitcase:* MANDELA. *The train moves on.* MANDELA *begins to walk.*

EXT. SMALL SHANTYTOWN. DAY.
> MANDELA *walks down the deserted street, comes to a shack and knocks. The   shack door opens.*

> MANDELA
> I'm sorry to disturb you. My name is

Mandela. I'm from the African National
Congress –

*The door is closed on him. MANDELA trudges on, comes to another shack,
knocks, waits. A MAN opens the door a crack –*

> MANDELA
> Don't be frightened. I'm a friend. My
> name's Mandela, from the African
> National Congress –
> THE MAN
> Oh, please come in –
> MANDELA
> Thank you –

He is taken into the shack.

CUT TO:

EXT./INT. SHANTYTOWN HALL (SMALL TOWNSHIP). DAY.
   *CAMERA TRACKS with men, women and children making their way
   towards   the hall.*

> MANDELA'S VOICE
> We're calling it the Defiance Campaign.
> We want volunteers. I'm the national
> volunteer-in-chief which just means I'm
> helping to organise. I'm asking for the
> first wave of protesters.

*CAMERA comes to an open window and through it we see MANDELA in the
hall.*

> MANDELA
> *(continuing)*
> We will call them *Amadelakufa*, which
> means those who are prepared to make
> sacrifices. Who are prepared to die. We
> need people who think they can put up
> with being kicked and beaten and who
> won't be provoked into violent action. I
> know I'm asking a lot.

INT. SMALL SHANTYTOWN HALL DAY.
MANDELA surrounded by a small crowd.

> YOUNG MAN
> *(rising)*
> Sir, I can't promise I won't hit back.

MANDELA

You musn't hit back, never. Wait for the
violence to come from them. I promise
you, you won't have to wait long.

YOUNG MAN

I would like to volunteer but I've been
arrested twice. The second time was for
hitting back. I kicked a policeman. You
know, sir, I've got a very bad temper.

MANDELA

So have I, but I'm learning to control
it. If you volunteer you must learn to
control your temper, too. These are the
rules: you have to remain non-violent no
matter what the provocation. You have to
dress neatly and cleanly, and there must
be no drunkenness –

A WOMAN, agitated and upset, stands –

THE WOMAN

Go away, go back to the city. I have two
sons in prison in Durban under the Pass
Laws. You want me to go to prison, too?
You want them to arrest everyone? They
are an army and they will kill us, you
are saying let yourself be killed –

MANDELA

No, no, you're wrong. Let me tell you
something. These past few weeks I've
been travelling from one end of the
country to the other, and this is what
I've learned. We are the army. I swear
to you this is the truth. Everywhere,
it's as if we're waking from a sleep and
understood that no one is alone anymore.
Yes, they have guns, but it has nothing
to do with guns. Throughout history, no
physical might has ever crushed the invincible spirit of a nation. And we are
a nation. We must pledge ourselves to
liberate South Africa – black, white and

yellow. And the lessons of history are on our side. We'll win because our spirit is invincible. And because our cause is just. We will win. I promise you.

(*He raises his hand in the ANC salute*)
Afrika!

CROWD

Mayibuye!

A moment of silence. Then someone begins to sing 'Nkosi Sikilele' i Afrika', until all are singing.

3

DEFIANCE

Apartheid was the Colour Bar made absolute. Social engineering of the most extreme kind now came into play. The triumphant Afrikaners, with segregation as their chief goal, set about classifying all the people of South Africa into their appropriate racial groups. In case natural instincts should in any way interefere with this programme, the government outlawed mixed marriage aand sexual intercourse across the racial divide under the Immorality Act of 1950. Thousands of people were affected by these laws; children who looked 'coloured' were reclassified and some were abandoned by parents; married couples were compulsorily divorced; there were many suicides. The next step was to confine non-whites to their own areas and allow them into white areas only when they were needed for work. Forcible removals – 'resettlements' was the official term – were a continuous process, and resulted in tens of thousands of blacks being uprooted and dumped, usually in the middle of nowhere. These displaced people set up camps in horrendous conditions: malnutrition and disease were rife – and all in the most prosperous country on the African continent.

Having separated the races and confined them to their own areas, the government now sought to control their movements. By a wonderful piece of doublespeak the Natives Abolition of Passes Act (1952) was introduced. Instead of a pass, the black would now have to carry a 'reference book' which was exactly the same thing. In time the term 'Bantu', which means 'people', came to be used by the government to mean all blacks. But perhaps the most infamous piece of legislation was to be the Group Areas Act of 1950, which may be regarded as the mainstay of apartheid. This Act gave the government power to decree who should live where. Its secret purpose was to keep white areas white: in towns and cities, the races were allocated their own separate residential areas. The whites lived mostly in suburbs; the blacks in townships or locations which were sited well away from the town, often surrounded by barbed wire and lacking the most basic amenities, including adequate public transport. To implement the

port. To implement the provisions of the law, large areas where non-whites had lived for decades were razed to the ground. Either these places were too near the white community or, even more cynically, were thought to be desirable for development – white development, of course. Thus, Sophiatown in Johannesburg, District Six in Cape Town, the Asiatic bazaar in Pretoria either ceased to exist or were moved elsewhere. In modern history there is only one other example of such brutal legislation founded on race – and that was in Nazi Germany.

Mandela described the policy of apartheid as 'insane', and there is a kind of neurosis that seems to motivate much of its impulse. Fear plays a great part. To most whites, especially Afrikaners who see themselves as the bastion of western Christian civilisation, there is the obvious terror of being swamped by greater numbers. Given the belief that the black hordes, the *swartgevaar* – the black danger – are an inferior species, the terror is multiplied. The neurosis extends predictably to sexuality: the black male is regarded in much the same way as Hitler regarded the Jewish male: a potent defiler of white, blonde Christian virgins. Yet the black female, prior to the Immorality Act at least, was treated as fair game. Bathrooms and lavatories come in for special obsessions. For example, in a building put to multiracial use there would be four sets of toilet facilities: one for white males, one for black males, one for white females, one for black females. If, horror upon horror, a black servant was found to have used the white master's lavatory, instant dismissal would be the inevitable punishment.

Of course it would be wrong to categorise all whites in this way. A small, a very small, minority sacrificed what could have been comfortable, prosperous lives to enlist in the cause of black liberation. The most active were often members of the white-dominated Communist Party. However, their Marxism encouraged them to analyse South Africa's problems in terms of the class struggle which, as has been shown, was repudiated by Mandela and other ANC leaders. The communists wanted to revolutionise the entire economic structure; the ANC were chiefly concerned with redressing the balance between white and black. Ironically, it was apartheid which drove the two together.

Some whites, of which Mrs Helen Suzman is still the most shining example, sought to oppose the government by whatever legal means they had at their disposal. Thus, Mrs Suzman sought and gained election under the banner of the Progressive Party, and was for years the only voice in Parliament fighting for a multiracial society. Others, mostly English-speaking, were opposed to Afrikanerdom but secretly condoned 'separate development', which is the euphemistic translation of apartheid. There were still others, non-Afrikaners, who actively supported the government and who were quite as extreme as the most rabid Afrikaner. It must be said, therefore, that the majority of whites – either fervently or not so fervently – supported the government and kept it in power. Instead of diagnosing apartheid as a disease, they came to rely on it as a prophylactic.

With hundreds of thousands of blacks crammed into townships and shantytowns, and constantly harried by the police, spontaneous riots and protests were frequent. But after the general election, the worst outbreak took place in Durban in January 1949. A full-scale riot developed out of a dispute between a young Zulu and an Indian which quickly involved more and more people. The Zulus' pent-up frustration, after years of oppression and poverty, was turned on the Indian community, the local traders and shopkeepers, who were deeply resented because of their relative economic well-being but who, incidentally, were also disenfranchised. The police intervened and there were 147 deaths including 53 Indians, 87 Africans and 1 white. A joint intervention by ANC and Indian leaders had, indirectly, far-reaching results.

The Indians had first arrived in South Africa in 1860 when they were imported as indentured labourers by English sugar-farmers in Natal. These 'coolies', as their employers called them, were despised by both blacks and whites and, being regarded by the authorities as non-white, were automatically discriminated against. For twenty years a young Indian lawyer, Mohandâs K. Gandhi, campaigned on their behalf and founded the South African Indian Congress in 1894. His philosophy of *satyagraha* – soul force, passive resistance – which was later to prove so effective in his own country, bore no fruit in South Africa. Over the years there had been little cooperation between Indians and blacks. Dr Xuma, President of the ANC, had formed a united front with them and the Communist Party in 1944 to oppose the Pass Laws; it achieved nothing. But Mandela was to be profoundly impressed by the action the Indian Congress took over the Indian 'Ghetto' Bill, which Smuts introduced just after the end of the Second World War. Two of Mandela's fellow-students at the Witwatersrand Law School, Ismail Meer and J. N. Singh, were in the forefront of the passive resistance campaign launched to oppose the Act. From them he learned about the Indian struggle against white domination and it was the idea of volunteers deliberately courting arrest and imprisonment as a form of protest that made the greatest impression.

Even so, after the Durban riots of 1949 and the joint attempt to calm the situation, Mandela and his colleagues in the Youth League opposed the notion of a united front with the Indian Congress. They wanted Africans, the vast majority of the oppressed, to stand up for themselves and oppose the government alone. The move towards an alliance was, however, strongly supported by Dr Xuma, who made a pact with two Indian leaders, Dr Monty Naicker, a Gandhian from Natal, and another doctor, Yusuf Dadoo, a communist from the Transvaal. The agreement was christened the 'Doctors' Pact'.

It was then that the young nationalists in the Youth League planned a *coup* against Dr Xuma. Anton Lembede had died in 1947 after a long illness and A. P. Mda was the new President, with Mandela as Secretary. A 'Programme of Action' had been prepared by the League which highlighted their dissatisfaction with Dr Xuma's old-fashioned leadership. Strongly African Nationalist, the document proposed, among other things, that new 'weapons' must be deployed: immediate and active boycott, strike, civil disobedience; it also called for preparations for 'a national stoppage of work'. Mandela, Tambo and Sisulu were deputed to confront Xuma in anticipation of the ANC's annual conference, at which they wanted the programme accepted. While they were forced to admit that under his presidency the ANC's membership had increased by several thousand, they still believed that if the ANC was to be truly effective it must forego the image of professional elitism and become a mass movement. The meeting was tense and unhappy. The young men finally tightened the screws and stated their terms: either Dr Xuma supported the Programme of Action or he forfeited their support in his election for President-General. Dr Xuma chose to risk the election without the Youth League behind him. He lost to the League's candidate, Dr Moroka.

It was an important moment in the ANC's history. A new tougher generation was in command, men who were prepared to act ruthlessly in pursuit of their aims. Skilled at the in-fighting which enlivens all political organisations, the ascendancy of Mandela and his generation of leaders marked the break with the past. Sisulu was elected General-Secretary by a single vote: he was to be the first occupant of that post to be full time and paid – £5 a month. Mandela was elected to the executive. Not surprisingly, the Programme of Action was adopted by Congress. Mandela wrote in the Youth

League journal, *Lodestar*, 'We have a powerful ideology capable of capturing the imagination of the masses. Our duty is now to carry that ideology fully to them.'

But they were momentarily pre-empted from executing their programme by an unexpected turn of events. An unofficial group made up of communists, members of the Indian Congress and Transvaal ANC, had called for a stoppage of work to protest against the banning of three prominent leaders. The stay-at-home was planned to take place on 1 May 1950 which happened to be the same day that the Youth League had chosen for its action. Outraged, the Youth League hit back. Mandela, no doubt because of his physique and fitness, was in the forefront of breaking up meetings. One witness described him as 'tough, yes, tough, and a hell of a temper. He stood no nonsense.' What seems to have angered Mandela most was the communist involvement. In *Lodestar* he attacked the party in no uncertain terms, rehearsing the argument that the workers were oppressed basically because they were Africans and only incidentally because they were workers. He went further: he prophesied that communism was doomed in Africa.

The Youth League's bully-boy tactics failed. The stoppage took place as planned and was counted a success: almost half the workforce stayed at home, but it was not altogether peaceful: organisers and 'scabs' clashed, and the day ended tragically. Some 2,000 police were on duty to enforce the government ban on demonstrations. When meetings became unruly, the police intervened and opened fire. Mandela and Sisulu were seen in Orlando doing their best to calm their followers, trying to persuade them to disperse. At the end of the day, eighteen Africans lay dead and more than thirty injured, including three children. 'That day', Mandela said, 'was a turning-point in my life, both in understanding through first-hand experience the ruthlessness of the police, and in being deeply impressed by the support African workers had given to the May Day call.'

Ironically, in the light of Mandela's attitude towards the Communist Party, it was a new piece of legislation called the Suppression of Communism Act which gave fresh impetus to the ANC cause. No doubt the South African government was encouraged by what was happening in the rest of the world. It was the time of the Cold War, the series of dangerous confrontations between the Western democracies and Stalin. So acute was anti-communist hysteria in the United States that in the 1950s the junior Senator from Wisconsin, Joseph R. McCarthy, was able to rise to national prominence and international notoriety as leader of a militant anti-communist crusade. His name became synonymous with political opportunism and public character assassination, and his activities were seen to undermine America's tradition of civil liberties. His witch-hunting was ended by the journalist Edward R. Murrow, who exposed McCarthyism on television. Then, in a rare move, McCarthy's colleagues in the Senate censured him for unbecoming conduct. To the Afrikaners in power, McCarthyism was the kind of vicious politics they understood and admired. The government regarded the Red Menace as on a par with the *swartgevaar* , so why not put the two together and club them with one instrument?

Under the Act communism was defined as any doctrine whose purpose was to bring about '. . . any political, industrial, social or economic change within the Union by the promotion of disturbance or disorder, by unlawful acts or omissions or by the threat of such acts or omissions'. Furthermore, the Minister of Justice could 'name' as a communist anyone he considered a communist, which in fact meant anyone opposed to the government. No charges needed to be brought or proof offered, and no appeal was allowed. The penalty was 'banning', which restricted the accused from leading a normal life in dozens of ways: the banned person was usually confined to one area and prevented from attending gatherings or writing articles among a great many other things. In the early days of the Act the restrictions covered one or two pages; in time they would fill as many as ten pages. A named communist was also liable to ten years' imprisonment.

The Communist Party, now outlawed, went undergound, but many members decided a better alternative was to join the ANC. Thus, the bonds between Africans, white communists and the Indian Congress were strengthened. In deciding to protest against the Suppression of Communism Act, joint action in the form of a stay-at-home was again called for 6 April 1950, the 298th anniversary of Van Riebeeck's arrival at the Cape. Anticipating the government's habitual response, the ANC warned: 'No physical might in the world can crush the invincible spirit of a nation', and added a promise to liberate South Africans, 'black, white and yellow'. The action was for the most part successful, but the real test of the ANC's strength and organisational skills was yet to come. When Mandela was elected National President of the Youth League towards the end of 1950, he and Sisulu discussed the next stage of the struggle, which was to be called the Defiance Campaign.

An argument within the ANC raged over what form the proposed campaign of civil disobedience should take. Was it to be non-violent or militant, should Africans go it alone, or would other races be involved? Mandela advocated passive resistance, because he saw no other way of opposing the military might of the government. And he came slowly, and even a little reluctantly, to the conclusion that other races as well as the communists should take part. In this way it was possible the government might be made to realise fully the broad spectrum of the opposition. The proposed tactics were put to the ANC annual conference in Bloemfontein. Mass protests were again called to coincide with an anniversary of white rule: this time the tercentenary, 6 April 1952.

Everyone involved knew there was to be a major problem which centred on the whole question of discipline. The ANC was going to ask volunteers to break the law in a variety of ways; those volunteers would then have to face inevitable police brutality. Would they be able to conduct themselves without retaliation? Was it feasible to ask people who every day of their lives were subject to brutality, to court violence deliberately and then expect them to react without hitting back? Was passive resistance an African reality? The ANC's solution was to appoint Mandela volunteer-in-chief, with an Indian, Maulvi Cachalia, as his deputy; their task was to tour the country enrolling volunteers, making it clear what was required and to set in motion a limited form of training in non-violent methods.

While Sisulu held the fort in Johannesburg, Mandela and Cachalia travelled from one end of the country to the other. In Natal Mandela met the recently-elected President of the ANC in that province, Chief Albert Lutuli, a newcomer to the leadership who supported the campaign. In Durban, Mandela addressed a meeting of many thousands. The list of volunteers was growing. They were to be called *Amadelakufa*, which means those who are prepared to make sacrifices, and told that in no circumstances must they retaliate. Drunkenness would not be tolerated. The volunteers must dress neatly and behave with dignity. There was a sense of excitement and danger in the air, a conviction that an event of enormous consequence was about to take place.

Meanwhile, in Johannesburg, Sisulu and the ANC President, Dr Moroka, wrote to the Prime Minister warning him that if the government did not repeal its oppressive and degrading legislation, the ANC would have no alternative but to instruct its members to defy the law. Dr Malan did not see fit to answer personally. Instead, from his secretary came an arrogant, dismissive letter questioning

Sisulu's right to speak for the ANC, and explaining that the laws were not 'oppressive and degrading' but 'protective'. They would, therefore, not be repealed; anyone encouraging disturbances would be regarded as 'subversive' – a word from Senator McCarthy's vocabulary – and would be dealt with appropriately. Sisulu and Moroka wrote again: 'We desire to state emphatically that it is our intention to conduct this campaign in a peaceful manner, and that any disturbances, if they should occur, will not be of our making.' The battle lines were drawn.

On the appointed day meetings were held all over the country. The people prayed for freedom. Mandela and Cachalia enrolled more volunteers. The campaign proper began on 26 June. Throughout South Africa the volunteers broke the apartheid laws. In Port Elizabeth, a group wearing ANC armbands chanted *'Mayibuye! Afrika!'* – 'Let Africa return!' – and marched through the 'Europeans Only' entrance to the railway station. They were immediately arrested; so, too, were Sisulu and fifty-three others for entering the Boksburg location in the Transvaal without permits. He was fined £1 with the alternative of seven days in prison. Before paying up he addressed the court:

> Our position has so worsened that today white South Africa has put in office a government which has closed all constitutional channels between itself and my people and whose barbarous and godless policies have shocked enlightened people all over the world. As an African and national secretary of the Congress I cannot stand aside on an issue which is a matter of life and death to my people... As long as I enjoy the confidence of my people, and as long as there is a spark of life and energy in me, I shall fight with courage and determination for the abolition of discriminatory laws and for the freedom of all South Africans irrespective of colour or creed.

In Johannesburg, Mandela addressed a meeting which lasted until the curfew at 11 p.m. The police broke up the gathering and Mandela was, for the first time in his life, bundled into a police van and driven off to the cells. He and his comrades sang 'Nkosi Sikilel' iAfrika', and gave the ANC salute – four fingers clenched denoting unity, determination, solidarity and militancy; the raised thumb stood for Africans in the south, a symbol of unity with all Africa. Once inside the prison a young European constable pushed one of the volunteers, Samuel Makae, so violently that he stumbled down some steps and broke his ankle. Mandela protested; the policeman, Mandela wrote, 'kicked me on the leg in true cowboy style. We were all indignant and I started a demonstration.' They demanded medical attention for the injured man but were told the request would have to be made again the next day. That night in the cells Makae was in agony. Only on the following day was he taken to hospital.

Throughout South Africa, over several months, the campaign gathered momentum and so did police brutality. People deliberately threw away their passes, defied the segregation signs in parks, railway stations and post offices. Europeans were terrified by this mass demonstration of black militancy and over the months there would be 8,000 arrests. At New Brighton railway station, on 18 October, two Africans were shot by a white policeman for allegedly stealing a pot of paint and resisting arrest. A crowd gathered, turned their anger on the police station and a riot ensued. Seven Africans were killed, four Europeans, and twenty-seven were injured. There were no police casualties. In Kimberley and East London twenty-five Africans were killed by the police. Demands for a judicial enquiry were answered by the government with tougher measures. Police activity was increased, the Pass Laws more strictly enforced. Civil disobedience, which meant black political activity, had to be crushed.

It was not going to be so easy. The campaign and the behaviour of the protesters had caught the imagination of people abroad. A United Nations commission was set up to inquire into apartheid. In South Africa itself liberal white opinion was firmly behind the ANC; some whites even joined the campaign. The government now had no alternative but to turn its wrath on the leaders. In police raids on 30 July, thirty-five arrests were made, including Mandela, Sisulu, Moroka, Dadoo and Cachalia. All were charged with furthering the aims of communism. Towards the end of the year over fifty leaders and organisers were banned for life; as a result the campaign lost direction and more or less ground to a halt.

Mandela and the others were brought to trial at the end of November. They were sentenced to nine months' imprisonment, suspended for two years. Judge Rumpff took the trouble to make the point that although they had been found guilty of statutory communism under the Act, their offence had nothing to do with 'what is commonly known as communism'. He added to the accused that he accepted 'the evidence that you consistently advised your followers to follow a peaceful course of action and to avoid violence in any shape or form'. These words could not have pleased the South African government. What pleased them less were the intelligence reports which told them that, because of the defiance campaign, ANC membership had risen from 7,000 to 100,000, and that a new form of protest was being planned.

FROM THE SCREENPLAY

EXT./INT. MANDELA AND TAMBO'S LAW OFFICE. NIGHT.
TRACK IN to sign saying MANDELA & TAMBO, Attorneys-at-law. Then
see interior of office and SISULU reading a letter to MANDELA and TAMBO
who are closing up the office for the night, packing their attaché cases, locking
the safe, etc., but listening intently –

                    SISULU
    (*reading*)
'In my opinion, Walter, 25th June, will
go down in history. There were three
thousand people. Africans, Indians,
Coloured and White. We carried banners
like "Freedom in our Lifetime" and "Long
Live the Struggle". The Freedom Charter
was read in English, Sesotho and Xhosa.
When the speaker said, "South Africa
belongs to all who live in it, black and
white. The people shall govern", there
was a great cry of "*Afrika! Mayibuye!*"
and so it continued after each section.
"All shall be equal before the law!"
"*Afrika! Mayibuye!*" "There shall be
peace and friendship!" "*Afrika!*
Mayibuye!" and so on – '

                    MANDELA
Go on, go on –

                    SISULU
Now, listen.
    (*reading*)
'And when the police came, armed with
sten guns, someone started to sing
Mayibuye to the tune of "*Clementine*". How
we wished you were all there, you,

Walter, Nelson and Oliver. It was so moving – '

EXT. STREET OUTSIDE OFFICE. NIGHT.
Under the dull glow of a street light, SISULU continues to read the letter
to MANDELA and TAMBO. All three are moved, excited.

SISULU

(*reading*)
'The police took everything they could
lay their hands on. Documents, banners,
posters. When it got dark they produced
lamps. And while we were being searched
the band played freedom songs and we all
sang "*Nkosi Sikilele' iAfrika*" – Walter,
you could feel the promise of freedom,
you could feel the promise of freedom in
the air. I hope to see you soon.
Yours – '

He removes his glasses and polishes them furiously. MANDELA begins to
make the first tentative steps of an Xhosa dance and hum some ancient
chant. TAMBO's face clouds over –

TAMBO

And we weren't there.

MANDELA

There shall be peace and friendship!

SISULU

Now I know why they banned us. So that
we couldn't be part of our own history.
(*he sniffs and replaces his glasses*)

MANDELA

These freedoms we will fight for, side
by side –

SISULU

It's a good thing I know you don't
drink –

MANDELA

– throughout our lives –

TAMBO

Are you drunk?

MANDELA

– until we have won our liberty –

SISULU

(*overlapping*)

He doesn't drink –

MANDELA

Afrika! Mayibuye!

TAMBO

Sssh!

MANDELA

I'm drunk! I'm terribly drunk! I'm
drunk on the promise of freedom. I'm
telling you, we've started something
that can't be stopped. The Freedom
Charter will start a revolution.

TAMBO

And we weren't there.

*Silence. For a moment, even MANDELA's mood plummets. Then, he puts
his arms round the shoulders of the other two and very quietly begins to
sing 'Mayibuye Afrika'. TAMBO and SISULU join in, harmonising. They
sing like drunks.*

4

KLIPTOWN

MANDELA & TAMBO read the sign on the second-floor window of Chancellor House, near the Johannesburg Magistrates' Court. The two men had qualified as attorneys in 1952 and set up their partnership in one of the few buildings in which Africans could rent office space. To outsiders they may have seemed an ill-assorted couple: Mandela, flamboyant, an extrovert who liked to live life to the full; Tambo, by contrast, more inward, a little cautious, less impulsive. But the common denominator of both their private and professional relationship was the cause, the struggle, the hatred of injustice, what Albert Lutuli called, 'the daily hurt to human beings'.

Although other black lawyers practised in the city, they were a rare commodity. Almost from the start Mandela and Tambo were besieged by prospective clients. The apparatus of apartheid is clogged with offences, many of them punishable by imprisonment. For example, to be unemployed is such an offence because the passbook requires the stamp of authorised and approved employment and without it an African risks arrest. To be landless, to brew African beer, to drink it, to cheek a white man, to live in the wrong area – all these are crimes which, Tambo wrote, 'no really civilized society would punish with imprisonment'. The result is that South Africa has one of the highest prison populations in the world. Each day the two young lawyers, again according to Tambo, 'ran the gauntlet of patient queues overflowing from the chairs in the waiting-room into the corridors'. He also observed:

Apartheid stirs hatred and frustration among people. Young people who should be in school or learning a trade roam the streets, join gangs and wreak their revenge on the society that confronts them with only the dead-end alley of crime or poverty...and if, when we started our law partnership, we had not been rebels against apartheid, our experiences in our offices would have remedied the deficiency. We had risen to professional status in our community, but every case in court, every visit to the prisons

51

to interview clients, reminded us of the humiliation and suffering burning in our people.

Mandela endorsed that opinion when remembering what it was like to appear in a white man's court. Yes, he and his partner were treated courteously by many officials, but more often than not they were discriminated against, shown resentment and hostility. It mattered not how expert or professional their conduct, they were made constantly aware that the higher reaches of the legal profession were denied them because they could never become prosecutors, magistrates or judges. They were acknowledged to be good lawyers yet had often 'to deal with officials [Mandela wrote] whose competence and attainments were no higher than ours, but whose superior position was maintained and protected by a white skin'.

On one occasion the hostility towards Mandela was official and unconcealed. The Transvaal Law Society, by presenting a petition to the Supreme Court, attempted to have him struck off the roll because of his part in the defiance campaign for which he had been convicted. Yet, dramatising the often baffling contradictions of South African life, it was the Chairman of the Johannesburg bar, Walter Pollock QC, who defended him. Judgement was given for Mandela: the Supreme Court found he was not acting unprofessionally to identify himself with his people and their political aspirations. The Law Society had to pay costs.

While contending daily with the practical consequences of apartheid, Mandela and Tambo now found themselves more and more embroiled in the political struggle. Mandela was elected President of the Transvaal ANC. He was also to serve as deputy to the new President-General, Chief Lutuli. It was at this time that Mandela's qualities really began to be recognised. This was the beginning of his ascendancy, the gaining of a national reputation which, given the circumstances, was all the more remarkable since the government was determined to crush the ANC and to silence its leaders. Mandela, Sisulu and Tambo, along with hundreds of other non-white leaders, including Lutuli, were banned. Mandela was prohibited from attending gatherings and was confined to Johannesburg for a period of six months. Even so, he continued to function at full stretch. Tambo wrote that Mandela 'trusts and is trusted by the youth, for their impatience reflects his own; appealing to the women. He is dedicated and fearless. He is the born mass leader.'

Behind closed doors, in secret meeting-places, Mandela and his colleagues continued their work. Despite the government's restrictions, there was still cause for optimism. The defiance campaign had proved that the ANC could command the support of large numbers throughout the country and 'the born mass leader' did not forget to extol the *Amadelakufa*, those who had made the sacrifices. The task now was to preserve against heavy odds the ANC as an organisation and, of course, to continue the fight.

From the government's point of view, with the collapse of the defiance campaign, it looked as if organised black opposition had been crushed. Yet, the ruling party was neither complacent nor idle. Dr Verwoerd, Minister of Native Affairs, and generally regarded as the most fanatic member of the Cabinet, began to think about taking segregation to its logical conclusion. To this end, he set up a commission to undertake a massive study of the reserves. He had at this stage no definite plan, but since absolute separation of the races was the ultimate goal, it followed that blacks would eventually have to be given areas of their own to govern. He may even have thought that a limited degree of autonomy would draw the sting of criticism at home and abroad. The reserves seemed to be the obvious answer and he eagerly awaited the commission's report.

However, Verwoerd's immediate priority was black education or, to be more precise, 're-education'. The defiance campaign had shown that the blacks were capable of militancy. The ANC leaders, although now effectively silenced, had in their public statements and court appearances displayed a certain unacceptable arrogance. ('Cheeky' is a favourite South African expression to describe any form of non-white self-assertion.) The blacks, Verwoerd argued, must be 're-educated' to accept their menial status in society and to rid them of any unrealistic expectations. He was, as always, perfectly frank. There was no point, he argued, in a black receiving an education which fitted him for white society where there was no place for him 'above the level of certain forms of labour'. The fundamental purpose of education, he said, was to 'train people in accordance with their opportunities in life'. His colleagues approved the sentiment and 'Bantu' education was placed under his control. He quickly decided that in future all blacks in primary schools would be taught in their own language, but if they went on to secondary school they would have to be taught in English and Afrikaans as well.

Government policy continued in other respects unabated. Forcible removals were on the increase; Mandela and other ANC leaders had their banning orders renewed, with Mandela being made to resign from the ANC; public meetings were broken up by the police; labour legislation came into force which was aimed at destroying black trades unions; on spurious statutory offences Africans were forcibly detained in farm colonies and made to work under hideous conditions – the catalogue of inhumanity was endless.

In the face of this continuing onslaught by the government, the ANC were preoccupied with trying to find ways of organising and rallying their members. Some of the ANC branches had grown to a size of several thousand during the defiance campaign and to call a meeting of the entire branch would undoubtedly draw a severe response from the police. In 1953, Mandela proposed his 'M Plan', in which he suggested that branches be divided into 'cells' based on a single street; seven cells would make a 'zone' and four zones one 'ward'. It was yet another attempt to build the ANC into a mass movement but one which could be easily mobilised. However, it was not wholly successful and for a variety of reasons. Most branches simply ignored the proposal. They were run by part-time volunteers who did not have the time to undertake the immense amount of work involved. Long working hours, poor public transport and tiring journeys to and from home, meant that people were too burdened by daily life to find the necessary evening hours for political activity. But the 'M Plan' gives a good indication of Mandela's political thinking: the ANC, to survive, needed the capability of calling upon the great mass of blacks who had no other voice to speak for them.

It was, fittingly, the educationalist, Professor Z. K. Matthews, a leading figure in the ANC, who first suggested a scheme that was to be of the utmost future significance. Because non-whites had no legal voice in any official institution, the idea was to find a form of gathering in which chosen representatives spoke for as wide a range of non-white opinion as possible. The delegates would come together and collectively approve a document which would proclaim fundamental goals and aspirations. That document was to be the Freedom Charter and it would be presented at a Congress of the People in a village just outside Johannesburg called Kliptown.

We the people of South Africa, declare for all our country and the world to know: That South Africa belongs to all who live in it, black and white, and that no government can justly claim authority unless it is based on the will of the people.

Winnie and Nelson
on their wedding day,
14 June 1958

The Mandela
wedding: a scene
from the film

Nelson and Winnie celebrating their marriage

Sharpeville: a scene from the film

The massacre at Sharpeville: a scene from the film

Sharpeville, 1960

Albert Lutuli burns
his pass book in
protest against the
Sharpeville
massacre: a scene
from the film

Mandela in detention
after Sharpeville:
a scene from the film

Violence or non-violence? While in detention after Sharpeville, Mandela and Sisulu are urged by young ANC members to take up the armed struggle: a scene from the film

Mandela and Winnie celebrating the end of the State of Emergency, 1960

Sabotage: the first act in the armed struggle, 16 December 1961:
a scene from the film

Blowing up a Boer statue, 1961: a scene from the film

So began the Preamble to the Freedom Charter. At the weekend of 26 and 27 June 1955, 3,000 people of all races gathered in the open air to approve the Charter. It had taken months of hard organisation to achieve. Extensive canvassing of opinion had taken place. People were asked what they would do if they could make the laws? How would they set about making South Africa a happy place for all who live in it? From the answers the Charter was drafted. Mandela and Sisulu, unable to attend because of their banning orders, approved the draft.

Africans, Indians, Coloureds and even some whites, including Father Trevor Huddleston, an Anglican and fierce opponent of apartheid, were present at Kliptown, representing great numbers in the country. The Charter was read in English, Sesotho and Xhosa. There were ten main provisions:

THE PEOPLE SHALL GOVERN!
ALL NATIONAL GROUPS SHALL HAVE EQUAL
RIGHTS!
THE PEOPLE SHALL SHARE IN THE COUNTRY'S
WEALTH!
THE LAND SHALL BE SHARED AMONG THOSE WHO
WORK IT!
ALL SHALL BE EQUAL BEFORE THE LAW!
ALL SHALL ENJOY EQUAL HUMAN RIGHTS!
THERE SHALL BE WORK AND SECURITY!
THE DOORS OF LEARNING AND CULTURE SHALL BE
OPENED!
THERE SHALL BE HOUSES, SECURITY AND
COMFORT!
THERE SHALL BE PEACE AND FRIENDSHIP!

Under each heading more detailed aims were listed. The goal was the redistribution of wealth, a welfare state which respected privacy and from which police raids were absent. And after each section was read the crowd shouted *Afrika! Mayibuye!* The final appeal was the most stirring:

Let all who love their people and their country now say, as we say here: 'THESE FREEDOMS WE WILL FIGHT FOR, SIDE BY SIDE, THROUGHOUT OUR LIVES, UNTIL WE HAVE WON OUR LIBERTY.'

On the Sunday afternoon the police, armed with sten guns, marched into the meeting. The crowd shouted, gave the ANC salute and started to sing 'Mayibuye!' to the tune of 'Clementine'. Speakers were searched, documents and even banners confiscated. But the delegates were undismayed. As the sun set all stood and sang 'Nkosi Sikilel' iAfrika' and the ANC band played freedom songs.

Mandela, Sisulu and Tambo, confined to Johannesburg, learned of what had taken place at second-hand. But Mandela was convinced that it was an event of outstanding importance in South African history. In *Liberation*, a left-wing publication, under the heading 'Freedom in our Lifetime', he wrote an article which included this passage:

The Charter is more than a mere list of democratic reforms. It is a revolutionary document precisely because the changes it envisages cannot be won without breaking up the economic and political set-up of present South Africa. To win the demands calls for the organization, launching, and development of mass struggles on the widest scale.

On 5 December 1956, at dawn, the witching hour for all totalitarian states, the police burst into Mandela's house in Orlando and arrested him. The charge was high treason.

PART THREE

WINNIE

FROM THE SCREENPLAY

SUPERIMPOSE CAPTION
1957
EXT. 'HELPING HAND' CLUB.   DAY.
TAMBO waiting by his car near the entrance to the club. Out of the club come two young women, ADELAIDE and FLORENCE. TAMBO kisses ADELAIDE on the cheek.

> TAMBO
> Adelaide, you look fantastic.
>> ADELAIDE
> Thank you.
>> TAMBO
> Hello, Florence –
>> ADELAIDE
> Oliver, I'm famished –
>> TAMBO
> Okay, we'll find somewhere –
>> ADELAIDE
> We could go to that café, you know the one I mean.
>> TAMBO
> Anything you say. Jump in.

EXT. STREET.   DAY.
TAMBO's car driving along.

INT. TAMBO'S CAR.   DAY.
ADELAIDE sits beside TAMBO.

> ADELAIDE
> *(suddenly seeing someone)*
> Oh, look –

EXT. STREET - THEIR POINT OF VIEW.   DAY.

They see a girl walking some way ahead.

                    ADELAIDE
        That's Winnie, that's Winnie Madikizela.
        She's staying at the 'Helping Hand'.
        She's from your village, Oliver –
                    TAMBO
        Madikizela? I knew her father –

When they draw level with her –

                    ADELAIDE
        Winnie? Winnie? You want a lift?

The car has almost stopped as WINNIE turns. She is beautiful and extremely shy. She smiles –

                    TAMBO
        Jump in.

She gets in the back and the car moves off.

INT. THE CAR. DAY.
As she climbs in TAMBO looks at WINNIE

                    TAMBO
        Winnie, I'm sure I've seen you somewhere
        before –
                    ADELAIDE
        She's been in the newspapers, Oliver,
        that's where you've seen her –
                    TAMBO
        You've been in the newspapers?
                    WINNIE
        I'm at the Welfare Clinic. I'm going to
        be a social worker. They came along and
        wanted photographs of some of us at
        work.
                    TAMBO
        Well, well, well. In the newspapers,
        hey?

He pulls into the kerb.

                    ADELAIDE
        Give me some money, Oliver. You hungry,
        Winnie? I'm starving, I haven't eaten
        all day. Come on, Oliver, give me the
        money –

TAMBO is searching his pockets.

>   TAMBO
> I must have left my wallet at the
> office. I haven't got a bean on me –
>   ADELAIDE
> Oliver!
>
>   TAMBO
> *(looking into the café)*
>   Wait a moment, our luck's in. Look
>   who's in the café. Go in, buy the whole
>   shop and tell Nelson he's got to pay for it.

INT. CAFÉ. DAY.
MANDELA is buying some sandwiches as ADELAIDE enters.

>   ADELAIDE
> Nelson!
>
>   MANDELA
> Adelaide!
>
>   ADELAIDE
> Am I pleased to see you! Oliver has no
> money on him and he says I can buy the
> whole shop as long as I make you pay.
>   MANDELA
> Have what you like, it's on me.
>   ADELAIDE
> Thank you.

She starts to collect up sandwiches, rolls, pies.

EXT. CAFÉ. DAY
MANDELA and ADELAIDE emerge. They carry a large pile of sandwiches,
cold drinks, etc. and make their way to the car parked at the kerb.

>   MANDELA
> I'm going to have to go back and wash
> the dishes –

They reach the car and ADELAIDE gets in and starts passing the food around.
MANDELA leans in at a window.

>   TAMBO
> We're supposed to be meeting in half-an-hour?

MANDELA

(*his real interest on the passengers*)

Make it an hour. Aren't you going to
introduce me?

ADELAIDE

This is Nomzamo Winnie Madikizela.
Nelson Mandela.

TAMBO

Would you believe it, Winnie and I come
from the same village?

MANDELA

(*to WINNIE*)

Are you related to this fellow?

TAMBO

Don't you know Winnie? She's always
plastered all over the newspapers.

(*Some laughter*)

MANDELA

The Welfare Centre. I remember. You
staying at the 'Helping Hand' hostel
with Adelaide?

WINNIE manages to nod. He smiles.

TAMBO

One hour. No later.

MANDELA

One hour.

TAMBO starts the car and puts it into gear. Timidly, almost surreptitiously, WINNIE turns to look out of the rear window to see MANDELA standing in the street. He, in turn, is watching her. He waves. Embarrassed, she looks away.

5

COURT AND COURTSHIP

Mandela was not the only one to be arrested and charged with high treason. In similar raids around the country the police pulled in 156 people of all races and flew them in military aircraft to the Fort, the old prison in Johannesburg. The non-white accused found themselves herded into two large cells. Men who, because of banning orders, had not been able to meet, now found themselves in close proximity for the first time in years. The whites were confined in a separate block: apartheid in all things.

Sisulu and Tambo had also been arrested; so had Chief Lutuli, Professor Matthews and other leading ANC figures, as well as Indians and Coloureds. Among the whites were Ruth First and Joe Slovo, husband and wife, both members of the Communist Party, and Helen Joseph, a British-born social worker and founding member of the Congress of Democrats. All three devoted their lives to the fight against apartheid. Ruth First, an editor of *New Age*, suffered long periods of solitary confinement, and in 1982, while working at the University of Mozambique, was killed by a letter bomb. Slovo, an advocate, was to become powerful in the ANC and a leading figure when non-violent policies gave way to an armed struggle. When they came into the old army Drill Hall, which had been turned into the magistrate's court for the preliminary hearing, all the accused were placed in a wire cage. Defence lawyers refused to represent clients who were being 'treated like wild animals'. The cage was removed. The feeling in the large crowd outside alternated between defiance and tension. There was the singing of freedom songs and general good humour, but the police were nervous and shots were fired. Twenty-two people were injured.

The treason trial turned into a long, complex, monotonous process which was to drag on for four years, but there was a positive side, since it acted as a catalyst for world opinion. A defence fund was organised which was actively supported in London, for example, by Christian Action under Canon John Collins. Even one or two Americans began to take an interest, but South Africa had not yet begun to impinge in any profound way on public opinion in that country. The South African government was determined to prove that the accused had participated in a treasonable conspiracy, inspired by international communism, to overthrow the state by violent means. Thousands of documents were entered into evidence, including many of Mandela's speeches and articles. The Youth League Manifesto and the Freedom Charter – 'the blueprint for a communist state', according to one government observer – were central to the prosecution case. Although the charge of high treason carried the death penalty, there was something ludicrous about the desperate efforts of the prosecution lawyers to make their case stick. From almost every point of view, it was to be a trial of patience.

The accused were eventually granted bail but because many lived great distances from Johannesburg, the possibility of visiting home or continuing to work was out of the question. There was much hardship. The years of the trial were a dreadful interruption of people's ordinary concerns, aspirations, ambitions. Tambo, for example, had wanted to become an Anglican priest and in 1956 was accepted for ordination by Bishop Reeves of Johannesburg. But the long legal process stifled that hope. So, he and Mandela continued their legal practice when not obliged to appear in the dock and Mandela ferried some of his fellow-accused to and from court. He was throughout cheerful and optimistic; by all accounts he exuded confidence and by force of personality – what may be described as 'presence' – instilled courage in others.

Yet, because the human being is alarmingly adaptable, the daily grind of the trial was accepted as a kind of unwanted routine that had to be endured. Despite the ordeal of having to give evidence and be cross-examined, despite knowing that the death penalty was a real possibility, many of the accused picked up the threads of their existence as best they could. In Mandela's case the public affair of the treason trial was, paradoxically, the most important period in his private life, for it was at this time that he met and fell in love with Winnie Nomzamo Madikizela. The circumstances were unremarkable: Tambo was engaged to a nurse, Adelaide Tsukudu, and it was they who, by chance, brought about the meeting.

She was barely twenty when Mandela first saw her, an exquisite young girl, modest and, in his presence, slightly withdrawn. She was born in Bizana, Pondoland on 26 September 1936, one of nine children. Her parents were both teachers: her mother, whom she described as 'a religious fanatic', taught domestic science; her father, Columbus, who had refused some minor tribal chiefdom, specialised in history and was principal of a local school. Because of his great admiration for the Germans, he insisted on the name Winifred, which in time became Winnie. Her African name, Nomzamo, means 'going through trials'. (Perhaps all African names are prophetic.) After the death of one of her sisters, Winnie remembers her mother being 'never the same'. She withdrew to dark corners of the house, praying silently, became physically ill and died. Columbus struggled to feed and clothe his large family and was the inspiration of Winnie's childhood. In his classroom she learned the history of her people, the Xhosa, and like her future husband was made aware of past glory and present injustice.

Even though she became head prefect, Winnie is remembered by a school-friend as being reserved and introvert. These twin strands in her character – natural authority and reticence – would be ever present. She would fight like a tigress for what she knew to be right, but seemed personally to lack confidence and, at the beginning of their courtship, was in awe of Mandela.

After qualifying as a social worker she undertook clinical training at Baragwanath Hospital and while there met Mandela. Tambo's future wife, Adelaide, was witness to the event. She, Tambo and a friend called Florence were on their way to a delicatessen to buy food. They happened to see Winnie, whom Adelaide knew since both were staying at the Helping Hand Club. They gave her a lift and there was much to talk about. Winnie came from the same village as Tambo, who had recently seen her photograph in a local newspaper when she had been appointed first black medical social worker at Baragwanath Hospital. In high spirits they arrived at the delicatessen only to find that Tambo had no money on him. Luckily, he spotted Mandela in the shop and told Adelaide to buy what she liked and to make Mandela pay. This she did and when Mandela helped her carry the food out to the car, he saw Winnie seated in the back. They were introduced. Of such moments legends are born.

According to Mandela's biographer, Mary Benson, 'What followed could not be called a courtship'; she reports Winnie as saying, 'If you are looking for some kind of romance, you won't find it.' It is certainly true that there was not much time for conventional wooing. Mandela, although out on bail, was on trial for his life. At the same time he had a law practice to conduct, his own defence to consider, as well as the innumerable demands made on him by others in need of help. And there were still the constant meetings involving speeches, discussions, decisions, besides the thousand-and-one unnatural shocks that political flesh is heir to. He also wrote many articles which needed research and care. Winnie, for her part, was still in effect a student and a conscientious one at that. Yet, in the accepted sense that the word romance describes a love affair which may be out of the ordinary and of a moving, passionate nature, then what followed is properly characterised as romantic.

Mandela was, as far as Winnie knew, a married man with three children and was devoted to his family. What she apparently did not know was that in 1955 the marriage had fallen apart. The pressure of his political activities had put unbearable strains on the relationship. At some point, his wife went to Natal to study midwifery. The separation was eventually formalised. Much of Winnie's initial response to Mandela was coloured by her sense of propriety.

She had, unknown to him, been in his presence on a previous occasion. Years later, in a series of recorded conversations with Anne Benjamin transcribed in *My Soul Went With Him*, Winnie remembered seeing Mandela for the first time in the Johannesburg Regional Court.

He was representing a colleague of mine who had been assaulted by the police. I just saw this towering, imposing man, actually quite awesome. [*Giggles*.] As he walked into court, the crowd whispered his name.

He was also a patron of her school for social work, so it was understandable she was more than impressed when they first met. However, awe gave way to panic when, soon after, he telephoned her asking if they could meet on the following Sunday. She was petrified and

... when I prepared to go and meet him, I took out every schoolgirl's dress I possessed. Nothing seemed suitable – in those days we had almost knee-length frilled dresses that made one look even younger and more ridiculous. And when I ultimately found something more dignified – it wasn't even mine. I felt so uncomfortable.

He took her to an Indian restaurant. It was her first taste of curry and it nearly choked her. Although aware of her obvious discomfort, he was unable to give her his full attention because throughout the meal he was continually besieged by troubled people asking for advice and assistance. At last they escaped and drove out into open country. On a perfect, cloudless day they clambered over the rocks and he told her the reason for his telephone call. Would she be prepared, he asked, to help raise funds for the treason trial? She agreed.

Superficially this episode seems prosaic in the extreme. Yet, it is an important moment, for, although he had only seen her once, Mandela was obviously attracted to her and, more importantly, appears to have perceived in her unusual qualities which set her apart. There were, doubtless, emotional forces already at work. From Winnie's point of view, here she was in the presence of a distinguished man she believed was married, eighteen years her senior, but vigorous, good-looking, impressive. She was, on her own admission, 'a little country bumpkin from Pondoland' and 'petrified'. What was she expecting? On the way back to the car she stumbled and the strap of her sandal snapped. She walked 'with difficulty, barefoot, so he held my hand as my father would a little girl's hand'. When he reached the car he said, 'It was a lovely day', and kissed her.

Mandela proved to be an unpredictable suitor. He would send a car for her which took her to his local gym. There she would watch him work out. Or she would accompany him to political meetings. She met his friends. Then, she might not see him for a week. 'Life with him', she said, 'was a life without him.' During this time, Winnie still did not know about his divorce: 'I couldn't bring myself to ask such a thing'; so that what happened next came as something of a surprise, to say the least. Winnie explained to Anne Benjamin:

One day, Nelson just pulled up on the side of the road and said, 'You know, there is a woman, a dressmaker, you must go and see her, she is going to make your wedding-gown. How many bridesmaids would you like to have?' That's how I was told I was getting married to him! It was not put arrogantly; it was just something that was taken for granted. I asked, 'What time?' I was madly in love with him at that stage, and so was he with me in his own way. It was such a mutual feeling and understanding that we didn't have to talk about it.

They were married at her home in Pondoland in June 1958.

Mandela was given four days' permission to leave Johannesburg for the ceremony. He paid the traditional *lobola* for his bride – cattle, not money – although she never found out exactly how much. There was both a church service and a traditional celebration and then they returned to a house in Orlando Township to begin married life. In August, in what had formerly been a Pretoria synagogue, the treason trial proper reopened and Mandela was once more in the dock.

The prosecution's case was never as overwhelming as the government wished. Since the preliminary hearing in the magistrate's court, the charges against fifty-nine defendants, including Tambo and Lutuli, had been dropped. Mandela and Sisulu, however, were among the remaining ninety-one who were brought to trial. The charge was still high treason although the alternative charge under the Suppression of Communism Act was dismissed by the three judges. The prosecution was led by Oswald Pirow QC, former Minister of Defence in Hertzog's Cabinet, and founder of the movement known unequivocally as 'Under the Swastika'. For the defence, a remarkable team had been assembled: Israel Maisels QC, Bram Fischer QC and Sydney Kentridge. The world's press was represented and members of the International Commission of Jurists. Once more Mandela's time was divided between the trial, his practice, ANC meetings and, of course, his new life with Winnie. They wanted a family and, over the next few years, they had two daughters, Zenani and Zindziswa.

Winnie wanted nothing more than to share fully in her husband's activities, to be his partner in all things. Gradually, she was drawn deeper and deeper into Mandela's world. These, then, were the years of her political baptism. 'I knew when I married him', she said, 'that I married the struggle, the liberation of my people.' She joined the ANC Women's League and the multiracial Federation of South African Women and soon sat on their executive committees with Albertina Sisulu and others. It was now she came under the influence of one of the most powerful and important black women leaders, Lilian Ngoyi, President of the League and later of the Federation. 'She made me', Winnie said, 'in the sense that I idolized her.' When the government extended the pass system to include women, Lilian Ngoyi was at the forefront of the fight. In 1958 Winnie, pregnant with her first child, joined in the protest, was arrested for the first time and, as a result, lost her job at the Baragwanath Hospital. Another profound influence was British-born Helen Joseph, whom

Winnie said she regarded 'completely as my mother, because of what she meant to me not only politically, but from a completely human point of view'. Both Lilian Ngoyi and Helen Joseph were among the remaining accused in the dock for treason.

With some of the leading ANC leaders still on trial, the government had every reason to look back on its years in office with satisfaction. By the mid-1950s the races had been more or less effectively separated. Black opposition, although never to be underestimated, had failed to have a significant impact on events. Dr Malan retired as Prime Minister in 1954 and was succeeded by J. G. Strijdom, 'the lion of the north'. The last vestige of non-white parliamentary representation vanished when, by gerrymandering, the Coloureds were removed from the common voters' roll in the Cape. They, like the blacks, would have four white representatives in the House of Assembly. In 1956 the Tomlinson Commission reported to Dr Verwoerd, the Minister of Native Affairs; the outcome was the idea of 'homelands' for the blacks, 'Bantustans', which, according to an official description, were to provide for the full political development of Africans 'including the option of sovereign independence based in their traditional territories'. It was yet another example of gross misuse of the English language. Bantustans were to be more accurately described as vassal states created as a sop to black autonomy. In 1958, after Strijdom's death in office, Verwoerd became Prime Minister; almost his first task was to steer through Parliament the Promotion of the Bantu Self-government Act (1959).

Another reason for the government's complacency was the scattered and disorganised nature of opposition both white and black. The white United Party split and its more liberal MPs broke away to form the Progressive Party. To begin with it boasted eleven seats; in the 1961 election only one remained, held by Mrs Helen Suzman. In Natal, the Eastern Transvaal and Pondoland, black farmworkers protested violently against the government's dehumanising policies. Towards the end of the 1950s there were urban riots and strikes. But the protests were never concerted and the highly-trained army and police were well able to cope. In 1960, however, the government's confidence was to be undermined.

Two events were to be of major importance in shaping the new decade. The first occurred in November 1958 when Robert Sobukwe split from the ANC and, together with a minority of like-minded men, formed the Pan Africanist Congress. Although he supported non-racialism, his true creed was 'Africanism' and of a purer strain than that espoused by the ANC. Since Sobukwe and his colleagues believed that Africans must liberate themselves from white colonial rule, any white influence was regarded as suspect. What Sobukwe opposed most strenuously was the influence of the predominantly white Communist Party in the ANC and its emphasis on class politics, which Sobukwe thought irrelevant. The split resulted in a wave of violent protests, called either by the ANC or the Pan Africanist Congress, the two organisations competing against each other for the minds and hearts of the masses. At the very beginning of 1960 there was an explosion of black fury in the township of Cato Manor near Durban, resulting in one of the worst riots in South African history. Nine white policemen were murdered after a liquor raid. But the climax of all the ferment was, as we shall see, to come some months later, in March.

The second event to take place with far-reaching results was the arrival in South Africa of the British Prime Minister, Harold Macmillan. He was greeted by his Commonwealth partner, Dr Verwoerd, whom he thought would have made a good impression at the Synod of Dort, a seventeenth-century Calvinist assembly which enshrined the dogma of predestination. So fervent and austere was Verwoerd that Macmillan was astonished to discover that he refused to have black servants in his official residence in Cape Town. But then Macmillan was confronting the visionary of apartheid. In their discussions no doubt Verwoerd tried to convince his visitor of the moral nature of South African policies. After all, Verwoerd was the man who, years before, had opposed Jewish immigration from Nazi Germany on the grounds that large numbers of Jews only led to the spread of anti-Semitism, which was not a good thing. Similarly, apartheid, in all its forms, was a Christian and moral policy for the sake of blacks as well as whites. Blacks must not be allowed a foothold in South Africa, he argued, because they could have no rights there and, as a result, must be disenfranchised. This, too, was not a good thing. The Bantustans, he explained, were where the blacks belonged. Total separation was the goal. On 2 February, Macmillan addressed the House of Assembly in Cape Town. Speaking in typically reasoned and reasonable tones, he made this memorable statement:

> The most striking of all the impressions I have formed since I left London a month ago is the strength of this African National consciousness. In different places it may take different forms, but

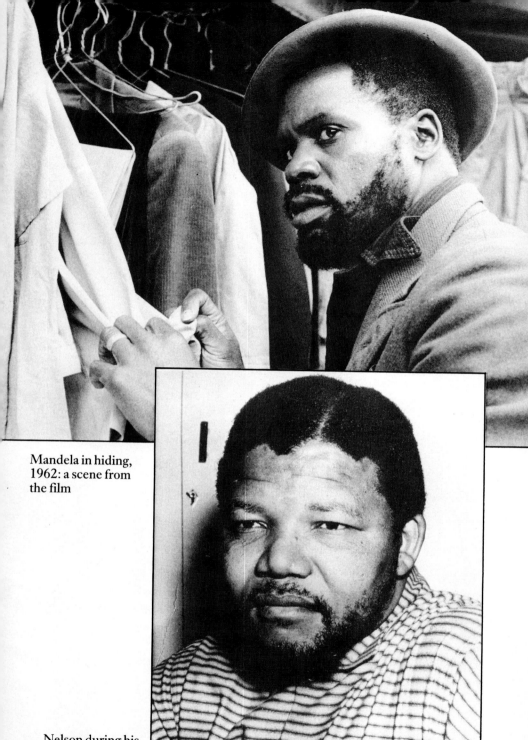

Mandela in hiding,
1962: a scene from
the film

Nelson during his
'Black Pimpernel'
period, 1961

Lilliesleaf, Rivonia. A rare moment of family life for South Africa's most wanted man: a scene from the film

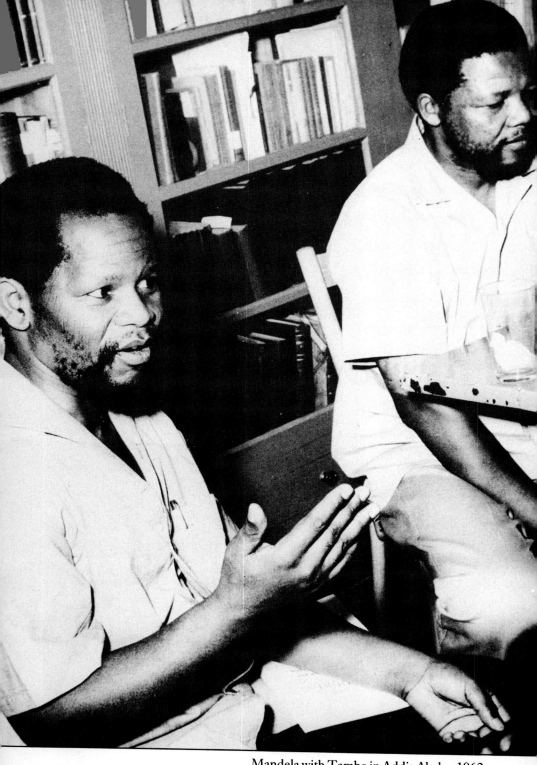

Mandela with Tambo in Addis Ababa, 1962

Algeria, 1962, at the military headquarters

Mandela, defiant, after being sentenced to three years' imprisonment in 1962:
a scene from the film

Winnie presents her pass book before entering the court room for Nelson's Rivonia trial, 1963-4: a scene from the film.

Winnie during the Rivonia trial: a scene from the film

Mandela in the dock during the Rivonia trial: a scene from the film

Robben Island

The courtyard of Robben Island prison. Nelson Mandela is amongst the prisoners in the back row

it is happening everywhere. The wind of change is blowing through the continent. Whether we like it or not, this growth of political consciousness is a political fact. We must all accept it as a fact. Our national policies must take account of it. Of course, you understand this as well as anyone.

But, of course, they did not. Macmillan's words were, as Michael Attwell observed

... prophetic, but wasted ... None the less, the full implications of what they had committed themselves to suddenly began to sink into white South Africa. There was no turning back, but the long, lonely years of ostracization unexpectedly opened up before them. Macmillan's words, pooh-poohed at surface level, struck deep, and sent a chill through white hearts.

During all these alarums and excursions, the treason trial dragged on. By the beginning of 1960 only 30 of the original 156 defendants remained on trial, Mandela and Sisulu among them. Chief Lutuli called for an economic boycott of South African goods. The ANC decided on mass demonstrations against the Pass Laws; in the tit-for-tat the Pan Africanist Congress called for its own widespread action. One of the places marked out for protest on 21 March was a 'model' township near Vereeniging in the Southern Transvaal called Sharpeville.

FROM THE SCREENPLAY

EXT. ROAD. EARLY MORNING
A BUS trundling forward comes to a halt. FOUR BLACK MEN in a line are
waving it down. One of them goes forward to the DRIVER.

ORGANISER
Morning.
DRIVER
Good morning
ORGANISER
We're asking you not to pick up the
people to work today. We are making a
protest against the pass laws. So
please turn back.
DRIVER
And if I refuse?
ORGANISER
Well, if you refuse, we are going to
burn your pass and that'll make trouble
for you. I hope we don't have to do
that.
DRIVER
Oh. Well –

The BUS DRIVER considers for a moment, then throws the gear into reverse.

ANGLE
THE BUS reversing. As it does so, it clears a road sign:

SHARPEVILLE
SUPERIMPOSE CAPTION:

21 MARCH 1960
Hold.

EXT. SHARPEVILLE STREET. MORNING

72

*Line of houses. (Neat, uniform, a model township.) Either side of the
street go men and women, knocking on the doors of each house.*

ANGLE – CLOSER
A WOMAN knocks on the door. When it opens –

> WOMAN
>
> Hello.

> MAN
>
> Hello.

> WOMAN
>
> Don't forget, no work today. We are
> going to protest against the pass laws.
> We meet at the police station.

The door closes. THE WOMAN goes on to the next house.

ANGLE – HIGH – SHOOTING DOWN
*THE MEN and WOMEN going from house to house. Behind them, people
begin to appear in the streets.*

EXT. STREETS. DAY
*PEOPLE walking, joined by others from houses, side-streets. The mood is
peaceful, high-spirited.*

EXT. NEAR THE POLICE STATION. DAY
*A LARGE CROWD (5,000 in fact) converging on the police station. Mostly
women and children. THE CROWD sing.*

EXT. POLICE STATION. DAY
Surrounded by a fence. THE CROWD are gathering.

ANGLE
*Unconcerned POLICE standing about, rifles slung over their shoulders,
smoking, laughing.*

HIGH ANGLE
*THE CROWD at its most dense: friendly, unthreatening. They shout to one
another. Some singing.*

INT. POLICE STATION. DAY
AN OFFICER on the telephone, only his uniformed arm and the receiver
visible. Across from him stands one of the ORGANISERS. Through a window
beyond him, the crowd.

OFFICER

(covering the mouthpiece)

> I'm on to Pretoria now, boy. They're
> going to send somebody down to talk to
> you about the pass laws, okay?

ORGANISER

Someone in authority, I hope?

OFFICER

Top brass.

ORGANISER

What time do you think he'll be here
because my people –?

THE OFFICER gives him a wave of dismissal and the ORGANISER goes.

OFFICER

(into telephone)

> I've got rid of him, sir, but I tell
> you, I'm surrounded. They're smashing
> the fences.

(a great cheer from outside)

> Yes. Yes. Must be about twenty
> thousand of them. Oh yes, they're
> hostile all right. Sticks. Stones. I
> would say I was under siege, sir. Okay.
> Thanks.

(he puts down the receiver)

> 'Someone in authority', cheeky bastard –

EXT. THE POLICE STATION. DAY
THE CROWD pressing up against the wire fences. They are singing.
Laughter, cheers.

ANGLE
Saracen ARMOURED CARS lead a convoy of police reinforcements, all
armed, into the station compound. The people wave and cheer.

6

SHARPEVILLE AND AFTER

The tragedy of Sharpeville on 21 March 1960 altered irrevocably the way South Africa was perceived both at home and abroad. What had begun as a peaceful protest ended in savagery and death.

Sharpeville was not the only trouble spot on that day. The Pan Africanist Congress had successfully mobilised large crowds to stay away from work, to leave their passes at home and to present themselves at their local police stations for arrest. At Vanderbijlpark 4,000 people gathered, at Evaton 20,000, and at Sharpeville estimates put the numbers at 5,000. The police were alarmed by the unusual size of the crowd. They had no experience of dealing with political protests on so large a scale. By ten o'clock in the morning, at Vanderbijlpark and Evaton, a baton charge and low-flying Sabre jets dispersed the demonstrators. At Vanderbijlpark the police alleged that a group of men hurled stones at them. They opened fire; one man was killed.

Sharpeville was different. The crowd outside the police station sang protest songs and was good-humoured. The low-flying jets failed to disperse them. In the light of recent events at Cato Manor, where nine of their colleagues had been killed, the Sharpeville constabulary became panicky. During the morning, reinforcements arrived, some in Saracen armoured cars. Some 300 policemen faced a crowd of 5,000. What happened next is subject to dispute. The police version has the crowd becoming restless and breaking down the perimeter fence, knocking over an officer and surging forward; the claim was made that stones were thrown. A constable then opened fire, which was taken as a signal for others to do likewise. Other witnesses, however, attest that the police response was more cold-blooded and that orders to open fire were heard. In the event, sixty-nine people died, including eight women and ten children. A total of 180 people were injured. Most had been shot in the back.

The government acted immediately by forbidding public meetings. Before the week was out Verwoerd banned both the ANC and Pan Africanist Congress. On 30 March a State of Emergency was declared. Over 30,000 blacks marched on Cape Town but dispersed after their leader announced he had been granted an interview with Erasmus, the Minister of Justice. Instead of meeting him, Erasmus had the man arrested.

Reaction in the world outside ranged from public statements of regret to mass demonstrations. The regret ('for the tragic loss of life') was voiced by the United States. In England, *The Times* railed against the 'wicked myth of Apartheid' and the 'blind obstinacy of Verwoerd'. The *Sunday Times* described the pass laws as 'an affront to humanity'. In Trafalgar Square, outside the South African Embassy, over 10,000 people gathered in protest. The consulate in New York was picketed. At the United Nations the Security Council demanded the abolition of apartheid. Britain and France abstained. More significant in South African eyes was the sudden withdrawal of money by foreign investors. Worse was to follow: gold shares slumped.

The white opposition condemned the government, who affected not to understand what all the fuss was about. Verwoerd used the recent troubles in Nyasaland, the Cameroons and especially the Congo to his advantage. What had happened in those places was much worse, he observed. After all, there whites had been slaughtered by blacks. In Vereeniging he addressed the faithful telling them exactly what they wanted to hear. They should not be upset. Law and order would be maintained. The black masses of South Africa were peace-loving ('and I know Bantu in all parts of the country'). The blacks were loyal to the government. The present unrest was the responsibility of groups of people who 'make use of mass psychology at mass gatherings, and by threats and other means' to seek their own gains. He sounded a defiant note: 'We do not intend to be perturbed about what is done and said in the outside world in all ignorance.' Foreign critics were simply playing into the hands of communists. His Minister of Posts and Telegraphs was less circumspect. He blamed Harold Macmillan, whose 'wind of change' speech he described as 'a message of death'.

True to his word, Verwoerd determined to crush opposition. After banning the two leading black organisations, he ordered the arrest of 18,000 people. Mandela and the other twenty-nine still standing trial for high treason were among those herded yet again into police cells.

Before their arrests there was just enough time for the leaders to consider what response the ANC should make to the government's latest actions. Chief Lutuli, who was in Pretoria as a witness in the treason trial, publicly burned his pass and called on others to do the same. He also called for a national day of mourning. He, too, was arrested. Oliver Tambo slipped out of the country to set up ANC offices in exile. It was clear that white South Africa was setting course for a police state and that more severe measures were bound to be enforced.

In the treason trial the lawyers for the defence withdrew on the grounds that it was impossible for them to function in a political trial during a State of Emergency. It was agreed that Mandela and Duma Nokwe, another of the accused and an advocate, should take over the defence. This they did while being kept in intolerable conditions in Pretoria Prison. The blacks were crammed five to a cell, six foot by twelve, with blankets and sleeping-mats crawling with lice. So bad was the food that Mandela complained to the Judge-President in the trial: 'Speaking with the greatest moderation it is no exaggeration to say that the food which is furnished to us in jail, My Lord, with due respect, is completely unfit for human consumption.' After a visit from the Superintendent of Prisons conditions were improved.

Mandela lived in the closed, isolated worlds of prison and court, missing Winnie and his new-born daughter, Zenani. To keep himself occupied he studied Afrikaans and prepared each day for the trial. The prosecution case was entirely dependent on proving that the ANC had advocated and pursued a policy of violence and was determined to turn South Africa into a communist state. Having failed to link the organisation to the riots in the defiance campaign – which must now have seemed like ancient history – they sought to indict the accused because they '*must have known*' that the ANC's policies would inevitably lead to violent confrontation.

Early in August, Mandela himself gave evidence and submitted to cross-examination; Winnie came often to court to hear the proceedings. Mandela's evidence was long and gruelling, ranging over his activities in the Youth League to the present day. Ironically, he was able to expound in public the aims of a banned organisation but his testimony is of intrinsic interest because it now seems so moderate and intensely reasonable. There is no more eloquent reminder of what he really stood for; of the many tragedies which enfold his life, the greatest is, perhaps, that no one had the foresight to treat with him.

He stated unambiguously that the ANC was not anti-white. 'We have condemned racialism no matter by whom it is professed.' He spoke of the demands for universal adult franchise and the willingness to back up that demand by exerting economic pressure. He hoped that would force the government to the negotiating table. And if the government refused to talk? 'We took precautions to ensure that violence will not come from our side.' But he was at pains to make clear, with some prescience, that he believed the government would not hesitate, if necessary, 'to massacre hundreds of Africans in order to intimidate them not to oppose its reactionary policy'.

In regard to the franchise, he spoke for himself: he was willing, he said, to settle for sixty African seats in Parliament as a step along the right road. In return, the ANC would suspend civil disobedience for, say, five years, a period which would be devoted to

> ... educating the country, the Europeans to see that these changes can be brought about and that it would bring about better racial understanding, better racial harmony in the country ... Then at the end of the five year period we will have discussions and if the Government says, 'We will give you again 40 more seats', I might say that that is quite sufficient. Let's accept it and still demand that the franchise be extended ... In that way we would eventually be able to get everything we want; we shall have our People's Democracy, my lords. That is the view I hold – whether that is Congress' view I don't know, but that is my view.

The prosecution had a hard time of it trying to find some way of making good the charge of violence. Had not the ANC supported violent revolution in other African countries? Mandela patiently explained that, in Kenya, for example, the ANC was concerned because a colonial war was being fought. He condemned Britain as the aggressor. Britain must leave Kenya. The ANC was not concerned with the methods used by the Kikuyu – by which he meant the Mau Mau. 'Our own method here is non-violent', he said.

Inevitably, Mandela was led into what was hoped would be the minefield of communist influence. 'Are you attracted by the idea of a classless society?' he was asked.

'Yes, very much so, my lord', Mandela replied. 'I think that a lot of evils arise out of the existence of classes, one class exploiting others.' But he pointed out that the ANC had no policy 'in any shape or form on this matter'.

What about a one-party system of government?

'My lord, [Mandela said] it is not a question of form, it is a question of democracy. If democracy would be best expressed by a one-party system then I would examine the proposition very carefully. But if democracy could be best expressed by a multi-party system then I would examine that carefully. In this country, for example, we have a multi-party system at present, but so far as the non-Europeans are concerned this is the most vicious despotism you could think of.

He could also have said that the Nationalist Party had done all in its power to ensure, in terms of the white electorate, a one-party system which had proved rather successful.

Referring to members of the Communist Party who had worked with or joined the ANC, Mandela's lawyer asked, 'Did you become a Communist?'

Well, I don't know if I did become a Communist. If by Communist you mean a member of the Communist Party and a person who believes in the theory of Marx, Engels, Lenin and Stalin, and who adheres strictly to the discipline of the party, I did not become a Communist.

What the whites in South Africa would never be able to understand was that blacks, in desperation, allied themselves to any country or political system which was seen to be actively opposed to apartheid. Chief Lutuli had said as much in evidence: when it came to 'East' and 'West', the ANC judged nations by their attitude to apartheid at the United Nations. This, I believe, is still a crucial factor. Western governments of even the moderate right seem to believe that being anti-communist is incompatible with vigorous opposition to apartheid. The notion was current then, and is now, that if blacks ruled South Africa, the country would inevitably become a one-party Marxist state. Furthermore, influential people of the right in America and Western Europe were justifiably angry at the double standards of the left in their countries, and that anger corroded their own standards of justice and decency. While the left demonstrated against the United States on a variety of issues, the right felt obliged to redress the balance by haranguing the Soviet Union. When there were no other causes to interest activists, South Africa garnered their attention. In the 1950s and 1960s South Africa was in and out of political fashion like a health fad.

At the end of August the State of Emergency was lifted and the detainees released. Mandela returned home to Winnie and the baby but the treason trial was drawing to a close and he was, once more, torn between Johannesburg and Pretoria, between his family and preparing for the final stage of the trial. That December, their second daughter, Zindziswa, was born. Years later, when in prison on Robben Island, Mandela remembered Winnie's patience, her love, her understanding.

In March 1961, the state concluded its case. The defence began what they thought would be weeks of disputation. But the lawyers and their clients were in for a surprise. The senior Judge suddenly cut Bram Fischer short and adjourned court for a week. On 29 March the thirty remaining accused stood in the dock and awaited the verdict. The Judge declared that the state had in 'findings of fact' failed to prove a policy of violence and that although a 'strong left-wing tendency' had been shown, the state had also failed to prove that the ANC was communist or that the Freedom Charter heralded a communist state. 'You are found Not Guilty', he said. 'You may go.' Outside the court, Mandela and his friends hoisted their leading counsel on to their shoulders and together with the large crowd sang 'Nkosi Sikele' iAfrika'. After four years on trial, five months of which were spent in prison, Mandela was again free.

FROM THE SCREENPLAY

INT. BEDROOM. DAY
WINNIE, trying not show her distress, packs things into a suitcase.
MANDELA comes in, goes to a drawer, and takes out some papers. She eyes
him for a moment. She summons courage –

> WINNIE
> Are you leaving the country to join
> Oliver?

> MANDELA
> No.

> WINNIE
> Then why am I packing these things?

> MANDELA
> Put these papers in for me, will you?

She takes them, her eyes never leaving him.

> WINNIE
> I didn't marry a man. I married a
> struggle.

He goes quickly back into the living room.

ANGLE
Beginning to cry, WINNIE packs the rest of the suitcase and closes it. She
pauses for a moment to regain her composure when she hears a great cheer
outside. Picking up the case, she hurries out.

EXT. OUTSIDE THE HOUSE – WINNIE AND HER POINT OF VIEW. DAY
She sees the CROWD surrounding MANDELA and SISULU. She sees
MANDELA near one of the cars.

ANGLE

81

She runs down the path towards the gate but the crowd is too dense for her to reach the car.

WINNIE

Give this to my husband.

She hands over the suitcase, which is passed from one to the other until it reaches the car. MANDELA looks back at her. Their eyes meet. But he is bundled into the car which immediately starts up and drives off. The crowd disperses quickly.

ANGLE
WINNIE watching the cars disappearing into dust. She no longer cries. Just stares. Expressionless, drained. Hold.

7

'THE BLACK PIMPERNEL'

In the eyes of the world Mandela emerged from the treason trial as the outstanding figure in the black liberation movement. Previously he may have been regarded as an attractive personality, conscientious and able but, perhaps, something of a lightweight. The trial changed all that. He had distinguished himself when he and Duma Nokwe had taken over the defence; more profoundly, his own evidence had revealed a cool, intelligent political mind. As Mary Benson observed:

> It was a question of growth, and all sorts of people quite apart from friends or supporters of the freedom movement suddenly became aware of it and began to refer to 'Mandela's increasing stature'. So it was ... when the ANC had been outlawed ... and it seemed that the movement must surely be numbed by the long imprisonments of the Emergency, that the time was ripe for a fresh lead, and a man was ripe for the moment.

Mandela was to be that man.

Secret plans for a new campaign of protest had already been laid during the trial and the opportunity to hold meetings and discussions had been unwittingly afforded the accused by the South African government. While confined under the Emergency, Mandela, Sisulu and others were able to meet daily and hammer out their ideas. If they had been left at liberty such meetings of a banned organisation would of course have been illegal and anyway difficult to arrange. As it was, in prison they decided that the ANC would go underground and that Mandela would lead the struggle.

For Winnie, the way she learned of her husband's decision was a moment of great anguish. She had naturally been overjoyed by the sudden adjournment of the trial, and could be forgiven for thinking that at last she and Mandela might lead a more or less normal family life. But when he returned home with Sisulu, Duma Nokwe and others, Mandela simply asked her to put some of his things in a

suitcase. By the time she had packed his bag he was gone. To Anne
Benjamin she said:

> I think he found it too hard to tell me. With all that power and
> strength he exudes, he is soft inside ... And then, before washing
> his shirt one day, I found a document in the pocket. He had paid
> rent for six months – that was very unusual ... Then followed
> extremely difficult days.

Although white South Africans may have been disappointed that
Mandela and the others had been acquitted, there were other matters
to preoccupy them. The long-cherished ambition of the Boers to be
quit of Britain was now the dominant issue. They wanted their own
independent country not with a Governor-General but a State
President. A referendum was held on 6 October 1960. Voters were
asked to record a simple 'yes' or 'no' as to whether or not they
wanted a republic. A majority of almost 75,000 said 'yes'. The
non-whites, of course, were not consulted. Elizabeth II ceased to be
Queen of South Africa. Her successor, C. R. Swart, the former
Minister of Justice, was to be sworn in as the first President of the
new republic the following May. South Africa, it was thought, would
remain a member of the British Commonwealth. But in March
Verwoerd attended a meeting in London of Commonwealth Prime
Ministers where it became clear that black Commonwealth leaders
would rather see the organisation destroyed than allow South Africa
to remain a member. Verwoerd announced that South Africa would
leave. The Afrikaners rejoiced, for they felt their defeat in the Boer
War had at last been vindicated. It was, however, the last time they
had any real reason to celebrate.

Meanwhile, the banned ANC had called a meeting in Pietermaritzburg. Since the defiance campaign of the early 1950s
Mandela, it must be remembered, had been almost continuously
banned. But because his latest banning order had just expired he
was able to attend the Pietermaritzburg meeting. His sudden
appearance was described by one delegate as 'electrifying'. He was
elected leader of the National Action Council and was entrusted with
initiating a new constitutional approach towards the government,
which had been unshaken by campaigns of civil disobedience. What
was wanted now, Mandela urged, was a National Convention of
blacks and whites. It was thought a new social order could thereby
be negotiated.

In the light of Republican euphoria, the ANC's strategy was

doomed. Verwoerd did not even bother to reply. It was, had the Afrikaners but known it, the final opportunity to find a peaceful solution to their age-old, intractable problems. Mandela, ever a political realist, went into hiding and secretly toured the country during April and May. With Sisulu, he began organising a three-day stay-at-home as a response to the government's unwillingness to deal. But he must already have known that non-violence was in its death agony. None the less, he hoped against hope that the government would see reason. He hoped in vain.

Despite his height and his celebrity, Mandela managed to elude the police who had issued a warrant for his arrest. He would appear and disappear suddenly, disguised mostly as a chauffeur. He was the authorities' 'most wanted man' and the press dubbed him the 'Black Pimpernel'. His chief collaborator was Walter Sisulu, the *apparatchik* of Congress, the negotiator, persuader and shrewd tactician. With his knowledge of the townships, of what ordinary people were thinking and feeling, Sisulu was the man Mandela trusted most. Together, under enormous difficulties, they set about organising the stay-at-home which was to culminate on 31 May, Republic Day. Mandela wrote to Verwoerd warning him of the impending action. The Prime Minister did not reply, except to tell Parliament that he had received from Mandela a letter which he described as 'arrogant'. Mandela also wrote to Sir De Villiers Graaff, the ineffectual leader of the United Party. Again Mandela warned of impending disaster:

> It is still not too late to turn the tide against the Nationalist-created crisis. A call for a National Convention from you now could well be the turning point in our country's history. It would unite the overwhelming majority of our people, White, Coloured, Indian and African, for a single purpose – round-table talks for a new constitution. It would isolate the Nationalist Government, and reveal for all time that it is a minority Government, clinging tenaciously to power against the popular will ...
>
> We urge you strongly to speak out now. It is ten days to 31 May.

The leader of the opposition, like the Prime Minister, did not reply.

Mandela and his National Action Council issued thousands upon thousands of leaflets urging people to stay at home.

LET US STAND TOGETHER, UNITED AND

DISCIPLINED. DO NOT BE INTIMIDATED BY POLICE
AGENTS AND PROVOCATEURS.
DOWN WITH VERWOERD'S MINORITY REPUBLIC.
FORWARD TO FREEDOM IN OUR LIFETIME.

And then the word *AWUPATHWA*, which means 'We shall not be
dominated.'

Europeans of all political persuasions took fright. The press,
including the liberal English-language papers, railed against
Mandela's call but ignored the fact that 10,000 people, leaders and
organisers, had been arrested without being charged; nor did they
report that meetings were banned, printing presses and leaflets
destroyed. Predictably Verwoerd warned all those, including
'intellectuals' and 'pseudo-intellectuals' in favour of a National
Convention, that they were furthering communist aims. His rhetoric
aside, he was genuinely alarmed. In an unprecedented display of
military power, with tanks, armoured cars and helicopters, he
instigated the country's biggest call-up since the war. Camps were
established at strategic points; hundreds of white men were sworn
in as special constables while their women spent the weekends
practising on rifle ranges. And yet, according to Tom Lodge in his
indispensable history, *Black Politics in South Africa since 1945*:

> ... the 1961 stay-away evoked a far greater response than any of
> the previous decade. This was all the more remarkable given the
> collapse of political organization within the townships during the
> emergency.

Unfortunately, Mandela's lines of communication with what was
actually happening were faulty. On the second day he called off the
strike because 'it was not the success I had hoped for'. Afterwards,
however, it became clear that hundreds of thousands had risked their
livelihoods and freedom to obey the call, and that there had been
a considerable disruption of industry and commerce.

In a secret press conference held at a Johannesburg flat, Mandela
hinted at what was to come: 'If the government reaction is to crush
by naked force our non-violent struggle, we will have to reconsider
our tactics. In my mind we are closing a chapter on this question
of a non-violent policy.' And later, in June, he issued a statement
in which he praised the response to the call for the three-day strike.
But he also gave notice of 'fresh plans for the opening of the second
phase in the fight against the Verwoerd republic'. The statement

ended with an unambiguous passage that has become famous:

I have had to separate myself from my dear wife and children ...
to live as an outlaw in my own land. I have had to close my business,
to abandon my profession, and live in poverty and misery, as many
of my people are doing. I will continue to act as spokesman of the
National Action Council during the phase that is unfolding and
in the tough struggles that lie ahead. I shall fight the Government
side by side with you, inch by inch, and mile by mile until victory
is won. What are you going to do? Will you come along with us,
or are you going to co-operate with the Government ...? Or are
you going to remain silent and neutral in a matter of life and death
to my people, to our people? For my own part I have made my
choice. I will not leave South Africa, nor will I surrender. Only
through hardship, sacrifice and militant action can freedom be
won. The struggle is my life. I will continue fighting for freedom
until the end of my days.

The decision to use violent tactics against the government was
neither easy nor sudden. There was evidence that young activists in
the ANC were becoming impatient, dispirited and, as a result, more
aggressive. In this they echoed to a greater extent the mood of
Mandela and his colleagues in 1944 when the Youth League was
founded, also out of a sense of frustration. Mandela and Sisulu knew
better than anyone that the leadership had either to accommodate
or assuage these feelings; if not, there was the danger of a breakaway
group running amok. To allow hotheads to pursue so dangerous a
course was to invite disaster. If violence was to be entertained, then
it was even more important to control the organisation.

But at the heart of the decision was the dismal realisation that
twenty years of non-violent protests had been answered with brutal
force, harnessed by a ruthless, highly-armed police state. Neither
the ANC nor any other black organisation had won a single
concession from the government; on the contrary, the Nationalists
had become more and more arrogant and recalcitrant.

With hindsight it is difficult to know what other course the ANC
could have followed. At the time the outside world was, as ever,
ambivalent. The South African problem was a unique one. It was
the only country in the world ruled by an oligarchy based on colour.
Yet, there appears to have been a deep reluctance to admit that the
blacks were suffering under a tyranny. The Nationalists were

perceived as a democratically elected party who inflicted the policy of apartheid by Act of Parliament and enforced that policy by their agents of law and order. A naive hope was nurtured abroad that somehow a more just society would in time evolve. But standards which might be applied to a stable Western democracy were misplaced. Apartheid was tantamount to a religious belief preached by bigots; it differed little from the racist policies of the Nazis. Pronouncements by Adolf Hitler could quite easily have been made by any Afrikaner leader, as a few random examples reveal:

'By defending myself against the Jews I am doing the Lord's work.' (Adolf Hitler)
'Apartheid represents Divine Will.' (D. F. Malan)
'The Jewish doctrine of Marxism.' (Adolf Hitler)
'The Bantu who advocates one man one vote is a Communist.' (C. R. Swart)
'The black-haired Jewish youth lies in wait for hours on end, satanically glaring at and spying on the unsuspicious girl whom he plans to seduce, adulterating her blood and removing her from the bosom of her own people.' (Adolf Hitler)
'At dances the Black native whirls with his arms around the waist of the White girl and what follows ...?' (Eric Louw)

One suspects that if German Jews had turned to violent opposition in the 1930s, there would have been widespread condemnation of their methods. After all, the Nazi Party had also been 'democratically' elected. Many Western democracies tended to support any regime that was anti-communist, no matter how foul, as they do today. And, of course, as far as South Africa is concerned, opposition to apartheid is tempered by 'strategic' considerations, by the vast mineral wealth of the country and the huge investments that have been made in its industrial and commercial enterprises. Yet, nor were many activists against apartheid blameless, including, perhaps especially, black African states. They, too, were selective in giving support to the struggle for justice around the world. They condemned the suppression of opponents of apartheid but failed to do the same when, for example, the government of the Soviet Union acted in like manner. The double standards on both sides of the argument led to a polarisation of attitudes towards freedom which in turn made a united front against apartheid impossible. Isolated and desparate, with the prospect of only limited help from abroad, the ANC leadership were driven to a course of action that Mandela, for one, was reluctant to pursue.

In 1961, a meeting of the ANC national executive approved a proposal from Mandela for the use of violence. Congress itself would not change its official non-violent posture but nor would it restrain those who partook in Mandela's campaign. A separate organisation was established to be called *Umkhonto we Sizwe* (The Spear of the Nation).

Mandela now faced hard decisions. What form would the violence take? Discussions focused on four possible choices: sabotage, terrorism, guerrilla warfare and full-scale revolution. Mandela argued for sabotage. It did not involve loss of life and, he said, 'it offered the most hope for future race relations'. Any of the other options were unrealistic. In view of the reaction to the stay-at-home, civil war between black and white was a real possibility and such a collision, if there was to be any future for South Africa, must be avoided at all costs. The aim was to destroy not only symbolic targets but also power plants, rail and telephone communications. Ultimately, what Mandela wanted was to undermine confidence in South Africa, to frighten off potential investors, to hit the white man's pocket in the hope of hitting his heart.

FROM THE SCREENPLAY

INT. ROOM, BUREAU OF STATE SECURITY. DAY
BLACK AND WHITE TRANSPARENCIES ON A SCREEN. ONE, OF A BEARDED
MANDELA.

> SWANEPOEL'S VOICE
> I want Mandela! And I want him now!

ANGLE
SWANEPOEL, a lieutenant now, angry and ugly, is talking to a group of
security and police officers, some in uniform, some in plainclothes, who
watch the screen.

> SWANEPOEL
> I have just been before the Minister.
> He has threatened me with the Prime
> Minister if we don't arrest that
> communist bastard. And I am threatening
> you with being back on the beat if we
> don't catch the bugger. Look at him –

ANGLE
ON THE SCREEN: MANDELA AND TAMBO.

> SWANEPOEL
> You see that other one with him? That's
> Oliver Tambo. Head of the bloody ANC in
> exile. And you know where that
> picture's taken? In Addis bloody Ababa.
> And you know where that is? That's in
> bloody Ethiopia and that means he's not
> talking to the Emperor Haile bloody
> Selassie, but to the terrorists, the
> bloody communist terrorists.

TRANSPARENCY OF MANDELA inspecting troops in Algeria.

> SWANEPOEL
> This is Algeria. That's where the Reds
> were fighting the Frogs. The Reds won.

90

So Mandela's not talking to the Frogs.

TRANSPARENCY OF MANDELA in London.

                    SWANEPOEL
And here he is in bloody London.
Talking to the Liberal Party and the
Labour Party and that means even more
bloody communists. All we need now is
to find him in America talking to Bobby
bloody Kennedy and you have the whole
bloody communist conspiracy. I want
Mandela! He's getting arms and aid and
talking to conferences and Christ knows
what. You circulate his picture to
every man on the force and the moment he
steps foot in this country again –

CUT TO:

EXT. ROAD, OUTSKIRTS OF CITY. DAY
A large limousine speeding along. It passes a sign:
                    RIVONIA

Hold, then

CUT TO:

EXT. RIVONIA FARMHOUSE AND GROUNDS. DAY
  The limousine enters the gates of the farm and makes its way towards
  the house. It comes to a halt near the front door. MANDELA (wearing
  the chauffeur's coat and black cap) gets out and runs quickly towards
  the door where WINNIE stands.

CLOSE SHOT – MANDELA AND WINNIE
They embrace fiercely, and

CUT TO:

EXT. KITCHEN, RIVONIA. DAY
  WINNIE, singing happily to herself, prepares meat for a barbecue with
  other WOMEN. She puts the piles of chops, steaks and sausages on a tray
  and carries it out into the garden.

EXT. GARDEN AND POOL, RIVONIA. DAY
  SISULU, and others, black and white, sit near the barbecue, talking and
  laughing. The group includes ARTHUR, KATHRADA, MHLABA,
  MLANGENI and GOLDBERG. The mood is relaxed. MANDELA and
  WINNIE are cooking the meat. The MANDELA GIRLS, ZENI, 3, and

ZINDZI, 2, swimming in the   pool with a couple of white children, playing boisterously.

ANGLE

A little later. The two MANDELA GIRLS, smothered in enormous towels, their teeth chattering, are being dried by MANDELA.

ANGLE

A little later, MANDELA, WINNIE and the two GIRLS, finishing their meal. The GIRLS snuggle up to MANDELA, who holds them close in each arm.

ZINDZI

When can we swim?

MANDELA

Zeni, first, you have to have a nap.

You too, Zindzi. Let the food digest.

(*Groans of disappointment*)

But I'll tell you a story. OK, you want
to hear a story? What story do you want
to hear?

THE GIRLS

(*making themselves comfortable*)

Makanda! Makanda!

MANDELA

All right, Makanda. Long ago, when all
that the eye could see belonged to our
people, there was peace. And then they
came and stole our cattle and our land
and put our men to work on their farms,
our women in their houses. These were
the evil spirits who came from a land
across the sea. But we fought them.
Our great leader, Makanda, followed the
tracks of the cattle they had stolen,
and carried the fight to their homes and
farms. Many of our people were killed.
But Makanda gave himself up because he
wanted to end the slaughter. But you
know what the wicked spirits did? They
put him in a prison, on a rock at sea, a
dark and evil fortress guarded by
monsters. And they call that place
Robben Island. But they went on killing
our people. So, on Christmas Day, he

and all the other prisoners escaped.
But, something terrible happened. The
boat overturned. The men swam for the
shore, encouraged by the great voice of
Makanda. 'Swim, swim to freedom!' he
cried, clinging to a rock until he was
swept away. But he didn't die. Oh, no.
Even now, on every Christmas Day, his
voice can still be heard, crying, 'Swim,
swim to freedom!'

He looks down at them. They are gripped by the story.

ANGLE

A little later. Everyone lies in the sun or in the shade, dozing. One of the black men sings a sad African song.

ANGLE

WINNIE and MANDELA lying side by side, her head on his shoulder.

> WINNIE
> Nel, shall I tell you something?
> MANDELA
> Yes, tell me.
> WINNIE
> You are in hiding, on the run, the most
> wanted man in South Africa and yet, this
> is the nearest to normal family life
> we've ever known.

(*She laughs*)

> MANDELA
> Oh my darling Mum.

He tries to smile. She closes her eyes contentedly. The man continues to sing.

8

VIOLENT METHODS

A white Umkhonto member, Wolfie Kodesh, was made Mandela's 'minder'. He came from a well-to-do middle-class Jewish background and was typical of those whites, many of them members of the Communist Party, who joined the struggle to change South African society. He had served in the army during the war, but afterwards felt unable to enjoy the comfortable life that was open to him. A man of infinite resource, he was small, muscular and practical. Detailed to look after Mandela, he rented a 'safe' flat in Johannesburg and there the two men lived. Mandela, unable to go out during the day, would rise at 5 a.m. and exercise for two hours by running-on-the-spot and doing press-ups. Kodesh, despite protests, was made to join in.

For most of 1961 Mandela and his colleagues planned the campaign of sabotage. Mandela longed for Winnie but she was being watched twenty-four hours a day by the police, who followed her wherever she went. She worked for the Child Welfare Society, visiting the townships and suburbs, concerning herself with the well-being of underprivileged children, so she kept her watchdogs busy. Nevertheless, she managed to see Mandela frequently while he was in hiding. Winnie confided to Anne Benjamin how the rendezvous were arranged. A friend would come and say, 'Make yourself as beautiful as you can. An important personality wants to see you.' There followed capers worthy of a B-movie.

> ... someone would come and order me to follow him in my car. We would drive a kilometre or so from the house, we would then meet another car, we would jump from that one into another, and by the time I reached him I had gone through something like ten cars. I never knew where I was. His hideouts were all over the country.'

Sometimes they met in the 'safe' flat or in the house of white friends who would arrange to be out for the evening. 'I had so little time to love him', she said. But they were able to enjoy more time together when a farm called Lilliesleaf in Rivonia, a suburb of Johannesburg, was made available to the Umkhonto High Command. Here, Mandela had his living quarters in an outhouse, and here the children came with Winnie; here, too, the plans were being laid.

The first acts of sabotage were to begin on 16 December, the anniversary of Dingane's defeat at the Battle of Blood River, the Day of the Covenant, a sacred anniversary in the Afrikaner calendar. An explosive device of primitive design was successfully tested one night in a deserted brick works. Afterwards, driving back to the flat, Kodesh remembered Mandela's elation. But there were still constant and worrying problems: security within the organisation, communication, the vigilance of the police with its network of informers. For Mandela it was a nightmarish existence, yet he exuded confidence and the very fact he evaded capture was an inspiration to his followers.

As the time drew near, the announcement was made that Chief Albert Lutuli had been awarded the Nobel Peace Prize. In his position as President of the banned ANC he had been kept informed of all decisions and plans by Mandela, who met with him secretly. Shortly before the sabotage campaign was to begin, Lutuli travelled to Oslo. In his acceptance speech he used this phrase: '... the goal of freedom could be pursued not only by representations and demonstrations but also by armed force'. It was as if, after fifty years of non-violence, he was warning that blacks now had no other choice: a new phase in the struggle was about to begin.

Because the Umkhonto cell in Durban acted prematurely, ahead of the others, the first attempt at sabotage took place on 15 December. A bomb was placed in the Bantu Administration office but failed to go off. The following day, however, the Day of the Covenant, there were successful explosions in Durban, Johannesburg and Port Elizabeth. The targets included a post office, the Bantu Affairs' Commissioner's offices in Johannesburg, an electrical transformer in Port Elizabeth, the first of more than 200 attacks which were executed over the following eighteen months in all the major cities and many smaller towns. The saboteurs were courageous and enthusiastic but frequently amateurish. Although Mandela had repeatedly made it plain that bloodshed was at all costs to be avoided, there were several attacks on policemen, informers and suspected collaborators. This resulted from indiscipline in the ranks and an unhealthy enthusiasm for violence among certain recruits. None the less, the scale of Umkhonto activity was impressive; its impact on the white population was, however, minimal. Mandela and other leaders began to envisage a protracted guerrilla war.

No armed resistance can be waged for long without foreign aid. Tambo had set up offices in London and in African capitals, but because Western governments rebuffed the ANC, financial and diplomatic ties were forged with the Soviet Union and its satellites. Once the campaign for sabotage was launched, the need for greater assistance was a priority. In January 1962, using a false passport, Mandela slipped out of South Africa and in Addis Ababa met up with Tambo. For Mandela it was to be a heady but brief taste of freedom. The purpose of the journey was to negotiate military and diplomatic support. To Emperor Haile Selassie's Pan-African Freedom Congress, Mandela made a long and vigorous speech in which he concentrated on the South African government's use of 'naked force and violence' to crush resistance to apartheid. He also talked of the external pressure, the efforts of foreign states, that was being brought to bear. But he also wisely observed:

> The centre and cornerstone of the struggle for freedom and democracy in South Africa lies inside South Africa itself ... We owe it as a duty to ourselves and to the freedom-loving peoples of the world to build and maintain in South Africa itself a powerful, solid movement, capable of surviving any attack by the Government and sufficiently militant to fight back with a determination that comes from the knowledge and conviction that it is first and foremost by our own struggle and sacrifice inside South Africa itself that victory over White domination and apartheid can be won.

From Ethiopia he travelled to other African states, then north to England where he met the leaders of the Labour and Liberal parties, Hugh Gaitskell and Jo Grimond. 'Wherever I went', Mandela said, 'I was treated like a human being.' The novelty of knowing he was neither hunted nor in danger, the absence of oppression and 'racial arrogance', of humiliation and indignity were exhilarating.

He returned to Africa via Algeria, where his host was Houari Boumedienne, then leading the Army of National Liberation against the French, and later to be President of the country. Mandela took a course in demolition, weaponry and mortar-firing and attended lectures in the strategy of guerrilla warfare. On his way south again, he conferred with Julius Nyerere of Tanzania, Kenneth Kaunda of Zambia and Oginga Odinga, leader of the opposition in Kenya. These six months away had been Mandela's only excursion abroad and he loved every moment of it. Before crossing back into South Africa, as if understandably reluctant to return, he paid another visit to Ethiopia to inspect the first batch of recruits who had been smuggled out for military training.

Mandela crossed back into South Africa at night and saw Winnie as soon as it was possible. A friend's house was put at their disposal. It was to be their last private moment together. In the weeks to come he reported to the National High Command of Umkhonto, then set off for Durban to see regional commanders and, later, Chief Lutuli. His disguise was once more as a chauffeur; his 'boss' this time was a theatre director, Cecil Williams. After meeting Lutuli they headed for Johannesburg. Near Howick Falls they were stopped at a roadblock. Carloads of police were waiting in readiness. It appeared to Williams that the authorities had been tipped off, for they seemed to know that Mandela, or someone important, was in the car. After seventeen months underground, Mandela was captured on 5 August 1962 and imprisoned in the Johannesburg Fort.

One of Mandela's associates broke the news to Winnie. She could tell from the man's appearance that something awful had happened. 'Is he all right?' she asked, and was told that her husband would probably be appearing in the Johannesburg court the next day. In her conversations with Anne Benjamin, she recalled:

It was the collapse of a political dream. At that moment I wasn't only shocked for myself. I was shocked for the struggle and what it meant for the cause of my people...
Part of my soul went with him at that time.

Mandela was forty-four years old in 1962 when he appeared at the Johannesburg Magistrates' Court. What with his banning orders, the treason trial and his subsequent life underground, he had known little freedom. Now, he was faced with charges that carried long terms of imprisonment. Although no one could have known it at the time, Mandela was about to begin a painful and harsh incarceration that, at the time of writing, has lasted twenty-five years.

He was accused of inciting African workers to strike and of leaving the country without valid travel documents but, because there was no evidence, the prosecution could not link him to Umkhonto. When he came handcuffed into the dock he was smiling and confident. One journalist remarked on his 'slow and dramatic' appearance, 'mounting the steps to the court like a quiet avenging giant'. The proceedings lasted a few minutes: Mandela was committed for trial. Winnie, in the public gallery, watched him led away.

There was a plot afoot to spring Mandela and get him out of the country. A warder in the Johannesburg Fort had been bribed. But when it was announced that the trial would be held in Pretoria, the plans foundered and came to nothing. Mandela told his lawyers, Harold Wolpe and Joe Slovo, that he would conduct his own defence. While he considered his strategy, events were taking place in the world outside that would have a direct bearing on how he was to conduct that defence and on the outcome of the trial.

Verwoerd had appointed a new Minister of Justice, a former *Hoof-Generaal* (Chief General) of the *Ossewabrandwag* and Nazi sympathiser, B. J. Vorster. Interned during the war, Vorster would make good use of his prison experiences when facing questions about the conditions in which black detainees were being kept. ('These people are living in a palace compared to the place where we had to live' or 'I had six weeks of solitary confinement when I was not let out of my cell for a single second', etc.) As minister, he determined to wipe out all resistance to apartheid, armed or otherwise. Under his humourless and cruel gaze the police extended their control over the population and restricted every facet of public and private life. If Verwoerd was the 'Apostle of Apartheid', then Vorster was the architect of the police state. He turned his attention to what Josef Goebbels called 'the instruments of propaganda' and brought under the severest scrutiny newspapers, magazines, books, radio and theatre. (Television was not allowed in South Africa until 1976.) White military service was extended and house arrest introduced: the first person to suffer under this latest contrivance was Helen Joseph, who had been bringing attention to the misery suffered by those banished by the government. Every night, at all weekends and public holidays, she was confined to her home. Vorster also gave the police the right to detain suspects for ninety days in solitary confinement without charge. (In 1965 the term was extended to 180 days.) The legal definitions of 'sabotage' and 'terrorism' were so loosely drawn that the police had virtual *carte blanche* to arrest whom they pleased. In police cells torture was commonplace and many men and women died while in custody. One victim was banned *after* his death to prevent statements he had made when alive from being quoted. And, extending his powers of 'banning', Vorster saw to it that a banned person was almost entirely isolated and silenced.

The International Commission of Jurists observed that these laws had not been surpassed 'by the most extreme dictatorships of the left or the right'. But Vorster's measures were effective in reducing the level of armed resistance, and the white population was reassured. With Mandela's arrest, protests both at home and abroad gathered pace. Vorster banned all gatherings which supported Mandela. In this atmosphere Verwoerd's 'bastion of democracy' proceeded to try its most famous opponent.

On 22 October, in Pretoria's old synagogue now used as a court, all those present stood as the prisoner entered. Mandela, wearing a jackal-skin robe, raised his fist and cried, *'Amandla!'* to which the spectators replied, *'Ngawethu!'* (Power! To the People!). Winnie, in the gallery, wore traditional Xhosa dress and her voice was as loud and defiant as any.

All trials conducted by totalitarian governments are burdened by the unspoken assumption that the outcome is a foregone conclusion. Although Mandela's defence was masterly, he was throughout confronted by the arrogance of the state and its unwillingness to yield on any matter, large or small, which might seem to dent its case. He must have known it was impossible to gain an acquittal for himself as charged and so decided to fight on political and moral grounds. At the outset, he made plain his position. In applying for the magistrate's recusal – a term used in Roman–Dutch law to mean objection to a prejudiced judge – Mandela said:

> I consider myself neither legally nor morally bound to obey laws made by a parliament in which I have no representation. In a political trial such as this one, which involves a clash of the aspirations of the African people and those of whites, the country's courts, as presently constituted, cannot be impartial and fair.

He developed his argument, asking, 'Why is it that in this courtroom I face a white magistrate, am confronted by a white prosecutor and escorted into the dock by a white orderly?' and continued with a blistering attack on the 'atmosphere of white domination' and the injustices faced daily by non-whites. He questioned the possibility of receiving a fair trial, but was at pains to pay tribute to the courts which, in many cases, he said, 'have upheld the right of the African people to work for democratic changes'. Although he welcomed the existence of a few honest and conscientious whites, he was not about to rely on them to change the grotesque system of justice under which he and his people laboured. In a passage that was to be remembered for its passion and simplicity, he said:

> I hate race discrimination most intensely and in all its manifestations. I have fought it all during my life; I fight it now and will do until the end of my days. Even although I now happen to be tried by one whose opinion I hold in high esteem, I detest most violently the set-up that surrounds me here. It makes me feel I am a black man in a white man's court. This should not be. I should feel perfectly at ease and at home with the assurance that I am being tried by a fellow South African who does not regard me as an inferior, entitled to a special type of justice.

It was to be expected that the application would fail. The prosecution argued that it lacked legal foundation and the magistrate agreed. Mandela was then asked to plead. 'I plead not guilty to both charges', he said, 'to all the charges.'

To prove Mandela's involvement with the 1961 stay-at-home, the state called for evidence from policemen, journalists, printers. But the star witness was undoubtedly a senior civil servant, a Mr Barnard, Verwoerd's Private Secretary. His cross-examination by Mandela was a fine illustration of white intransigence and the totalitarian mentality. It centred on the letter written by Mandela to Verwoerd demanding a National Convention in May 1961. Here are some examples from Barnard's evidence:

MANDELA: Did he [Verwoerd] reply to this letter?

BARNARD: He did not reply to the writer.

MANDELA: He did not reply to the letter. Now, will you agree that this letter raises matters of vital concern to the vast majority of the citizens of this country?

BARNARD: I do not agree.

MANDELA: You don't agree? You don't agree that the question of human rights, of civil liberties, is a matter of vital importance to the African people?

BARNARD: Yes, that is so, indeed.

MANDELA: Are these things mentioned here?

BARNARD: Yes, I think so.

Mandela then made Barnard admit that the letter dealt with freedom and civil liberties, and that it also drew attention to the fact that blacks had no parliamentary representation and no vote.

MANDELA: Would you agree with me that in any civilized country in the world it would be at least most scandalous for a Prime Minister to fail to reply to a letter raising vital issues affecting the majority of the citizens of that country. Would you agree with that?

BARNARD: I don't agree with that.

MANDELA: You don't agree that it would be irregular for a Prime Minister to ignore a letter raising vital issues affecting the vast majority of the citizens of that country?

BARNARD: This letter has not been ignored by the Prime Minister.

A chink of light, one might think, so Mandela steered Barnard into defining Verwoerd's response. No, Barnard agreed, the Prime Minister certainly had not acknowledged the letter. How then could Barnard say it had not been ignored? The letter, Barnard explained, was referred to the appropriate department, in this case the Department of Justice. Well, why had the Minister of Justice failed to acknowledge or reply?

BARNARD: When a letter is replied to and whether it should be replied to, depends on the contents of the letter in many instances.

MANDELA: My question is, can you explain to me why I was not favoured with the courtesy of an acknowledgement of the letter, irrespective of what the Prime Minister is going to do about it? Why was I not favoured with this courtesy?

BARNARD: Because of the contents of this letter.

MANDELA: Because it raises vital issues?

BARNARD: Because of the contents of the letter.

MANDELA: I see. This is not the type of thing the Prime Minister would ever consider responding to?

BARNARD: The Prime Minister did respond.

After the letter was read out, Mandela asked Barnard to verify that it was indeed the letter received by Verwoerd. Barnard's reply was, to say the least, oblique. He didn't think it was the letter, he said. 'I think it shouldn't be called a letter in the first instance, but an accumulation of threats.'

Another witness, Warrant Officer Baardman of the Bloemfontein Special Branch, lacked Barnard's civil service finesse but seemed to adopt the approach of a logical positivist. The cross-examination turned on the concept of a National Convention. Wasn't it true, Mandela asked, that the present constitution of South Africa was passed at a National Convention representing whites only?

BAARDMAN: I don't know, I was not there.
MANDELA: But from your knowledge?
BAARDMAN: I don't know, I was not there.
MANDELA: You don't know at all?
BAARDMAN: No, I don't know.
MANDELA: You want this Court to believe that, that you don't know?
BAARDMAN: I don't know, I was not there.
MANDELA: Just let me put the question. You don't know that the National Convention in 1909 was a convention of whites only?
BAARDMAN: I don't know, I was not there.

The prosecution case took three days to present and ended with a demand to find Mandela guilty. The magistrate asked the accused, 'Have you anything to say?'

MANDELA: Your Worship, I submit that I am guilty of no crime.
MAGISTRATE: Is that all you have to say?
MANDELA: Your Worship, with respect, if I had something more to say, I would have said it.

Mandela was found guilty on both counts. In the magistrate's opinion, Mandela led and instigated the stay-at-home in 1961. He was the figurehead, the mouthpiece and the brains behind the organisation. He acted unlawfully and undemocratically. Worse, he showed no remorse but indeed seemed proud of his achievements and had made it clear that he would continue his activities no matter what sentence was passed upon him. The courts were concerned with law and order not politics. Without law and order there would be anarchy.

Mandela was then asked to address the court in mitigation of sentence. His speech was long, complex, closely argued. It was never a plea for mitigation but the political creed of a greatly gifted man

Life imprisonment
on Robben Island,
mid-1960s: a scene
from the film

Sisulu and Mandela breaking stones on Robben Island during their life sentence: a scene from the film

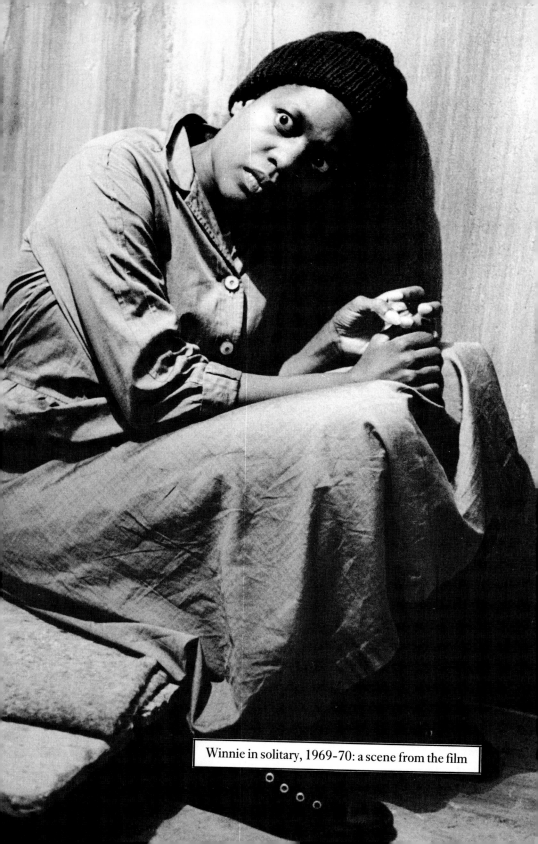

Winnie in solitary, 1969-70: a scene from the film

Winnie visits Nelson on Robben Island: a scene from the film

The tragedy at Soweto, 1976

Soweto. The poster above reads 'Away with Kaferkaans' – a play on the derogatory word for black, 'Kaffir', and Afrikaans, against which the young people were protesting

Soweto

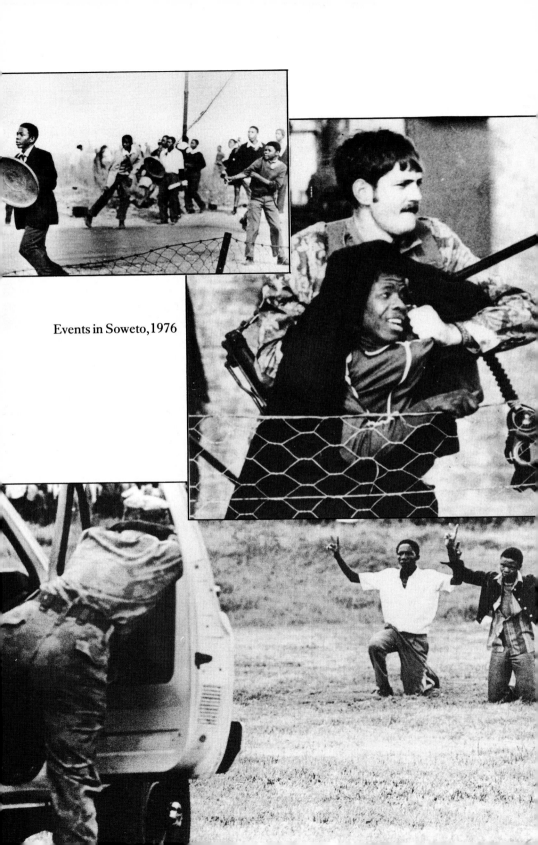

Events in Soweto, 1976

Soweto

Winnie mourns at the funeral of 59 children killed in the Soweto uprising: a scene from the film

Zindzi in Soweto, 1985: a scene from the film

Zindzi Mandela, after reading her father's reply to Botha's conditional offer of freedom: Jubulani Stadium, Soweto, 1985

who had devoted his entire adult life to fighting oppression and injustice. Every aspect of South African politics was thoroughly exposed: white domination, the development of black opposition, his own part in it, the mounting violence of the state. He savaged the government's refusal to deal with responsible black leaders. Blacks had no legal means of protest. They had been forced by a despicable and brutal system into adopting the only methods available. He concluded:

> I have done my duty to my people and to South Africa. I have no doubt that posterity will pronounce that I was innocent and that the criminals that should have been brought before this Court are the members of the Verwoerd Government.

On 7 November 1962, Mandela was sentenced to three years' imprisonment on the charge of incitement to strike and two years for leaving the country without valid travel documents. As he was taken down from the dock he cried three times, *'Amandla!'* and three times came the response, *'Ngawethu!'* When the police van carrying him off to prison left the court, the crowd ignored Vorster's prohibitions and marched through the streets singing, *'Tshotsholoza Mandela'* – 'Struggle on, Mandela'.

'I will continue the fight as I have in all ways done in the past', Winnie said. With her husband beginning his sentence in Pretoria Central Prison, sewing mailbags and in solitary confinement, Winnie edged slowly into the spotlight. Since her marriage to Mandela in 1958, she had known little of what may be thought of as a normal existence. For most of their married life her husband had either been on trial or in hiding. Her daily expectation was danger and anxiety, the whispered message, the secret meeting, the terrible strain of not knowing where her husband was or what was happening to him. She had always shown passion for the cause and demonstrated political intelligence. By choice and circumstance she had remained in Mandela's shadow. Now, her life was to change. At first she would be perceived as little more than a symbolic figure, a wife fighting to keep her imprisoned husband's name alive. But the relentless persecution of her by the state, her own remarkable qualities of endurance and courage, gradually transformed her into a formidable opponent of the regime in her own right. From the moment Mandela began his sentence she willingly took on the role as the heroine of black resistance. 'Suffering is not enough', she said. 'We must struggle.' It was like a prophecy doomed to come true.

From Pretoria Mandela was transferred to the most dreaded prison in South Africa, the penal settlement of Robben Island, five miles off Cape Town. There he joined Robert Sobukwe, the leader of the Pan Africanist Congress, and other enemies of apartheid. And on the mainland the police continued to arrest men and women in their hundreds, hold them for ninety days in detention where they would be questioned, tortured and, in some cases, murdered. In 1962 Walter Sisulu was arrested six times. He, like Mandela, was charged with incitement to strike and of furthering the aims of the ANC. His case dragged on for nearly five months and during the period he was allowed out on bail. In March 1963 he was sentenced to six years' imprisonment; bail was withdrawn but reinstated by the Supreme Court. Sisulu realised his time had run out and, in April, he went underground to join the Umkhonto High Command. Barely three months later, on 12 July, his days as an outlaw ended.

Sisulu's arrest with eight other leading activists represented a spectacular success for the South African security forces. To this day it is not known who gave the police the address of Lilliesleaf Farm in Rivonia. Three possibilities have been offered: a prisoner was made to speak under torture, an informer was at work, or some of those involved in Umkhonto had become careless about security. By whatever means the information was obtained, the police had the address of the house where the country's most wanted men met. It was also the place, of course, where Mandela had stayed and worked while underground. The pickings were rich. Among the prisoners were two whites, Lionel 'Rusty' Bernstein and Dennis Goldberg; the blacks included Sisulu, Govan Mbeki, Raymond Mhlaba, Elias Motsoaledi and Andrew Mlangeni; and there was one Indian, Ahmed Kathrada. But more pleasing to the police was the discovery of a vast store of documents, some of which seemed to tie Mandela to terrorism.

FROM THE SCREENPLAY

INT. PRISON INTERVIEW ROOM. DAY
The Rivonia accused are led into the interview room where their lawyers,
FISCHER and JOFFE, wait. The sound of footsteps and banging doors. TWO
WARDERS bring in MANDELA wearing prison uniform — shorts and shirt.
He stops, looks at the others, then breaks into a huge smile.

MANDELA

It's nice to be among friends again.

SISULU is already out of his chair. He and MANDELA go towards each other
and embrace; the others, including the two lawyers, gather round them,
joining in the embrace like footballers after a goal.

WARDER

No touching! No touching!

They ignore him.

ALL

(*Simultaneously*)
>   – Nelson, Nelson –
>   – It's good to see you –
>   – You've lost weight –
>   – Are they treating you all right? –
>   – How are you?
>   – It's great seeing you –
>   – Are you keeping fit?
>   – I'm so happy to see you –

FISCHER

(*indicating the door*)
>   Thank you, Warder

WARDER

(*going*)
>   Right, Mr Fischer.

ANGLE
THE WARDERS, realising they have no option, leave the room and lock the

105

door from the outside. The sound of keys in locks dampens the excitement.

FISCHER

Come on, we've got work to do.

They all take their places at the table; as they do so, MANDELA holds SISULU back.

ANGLE

MANDELA

How are you?

SISULU

I'm fine. Fine.

MANDELA

How's Albertina?

SISULU

Albertina's fine. And Winnie's fine
too. They're strong.

(They smile.)

ANGLE

MANDELA and SISULU join the others at the table.

FISCHER

First of all, Nelson, I don't know how
much you know –

MANDELA

Bram, I know about Rivonia. I know they
say they've found evidence. They took
great pleasure in telling me I was for
the high jump. But what I don't know
are the charges.

JOFFE

Nobody knows. But there have been leaks
to the press –

FISCHER

Look, you can be certain of one thing.
All of you are going to be charged with
being involved in sabotage and guerrilla
warfare –

SISULU

We never decided on guerrilla warfare.
On the contrary, our policy was not to
endanger human life –

FISCHER

Okay, but as sure as you're sitting
there, they're going to say you wanted

to bring down the government by violent revolution.

JOFFE

And, in your case, Nelson, I'm sure
they're going to say that your trip
abroad was to raise funds for the struggle.

FISCHER

Yes, and of course, communism's bound to
come into it somewhere.

MLANGENI

They'll stop at nothing.

A little laughter; pause.

FISCHER

Look. There's no point in trying to
bluff ourselves. Whatever the charges,
they're going to carry the death
penalty. The government wants a
hanging.

(*Silence; then, business-like*)

We've got a helluva fight on our hands.
So, what I suggest is we attack each
charge in detail. My information is
there may be as many as two hundred
separate allegations of sabotage. This
means we have to examine each one under
a microscope. Dates, times, where you
were, witnesses –

MANDELA

Can I say something? Obviously, I
haven't had a chance to discuss this
with the others, but I'll tell you what
I feel. I think we have a wonderful
opportunity here. I don't think we
should fig*h*t them on legal grounds.

FISCHER

But, Nelson, we're talking about the
death penalty. We *must* defend you on
legal grounds –

MANDELA

No. if they want to hang us, they'll
hang us. So let's make the best of it.
We have to turn this into a political
trial.

General approval from the others.

> SISULU
>
> We've been talking about this as well,
> Bram, and I think I can say we're one
> hundred per cent behind Nelson. This is
> a chance to use the court as a platform,
> to make known what we believe in –
>
> MANDELA

Right –

> SISULU

(continuing)

> And we'll be talking to the whole world.
> And we can defy the government in open
> court. We can speak with pride –
>
> MANDELA
>
> We can explain why we were driven to do
> what we did. We've nothing to be
> ashamed of, we had no alternative.
> That's what I want to say.
>
> SISULU
>
> And I think we should go further. We
> should admit that we want to bring the
> government down. And tell them why.
>
> MANDELA
>
> Agreed. We should say, yes, we took
> part in acts of sabotage. Yes, I went
> abroad to get help for the struggle.
> Our only defence is attack. It's no
> good fighting them in law. We have to
> fight them politically. Not on their
> terms but on ours.

Silence.

> FISCHER
>
> You realise that's like putting the
> noose round your own necks.

Silence.

9

LIFE SENTENCE

To begin with the Rivonia accused were held under the ninety-day detention law. In solitary confinement they were isolated from their families, friends and, perhaps more importantly in the immediate circumstances, their lawyers. Nevertheless a legal team was appointed, since it was obvious that the men would in time be brought to trial. Bram Fischer QC was to lead Vernon Berrange, Arthur Chaskalson and George Bizos. The attorney was Joel Joffe. But the government, in an arrogant display of power, allowed no one on the outside to know who precisely the accused were or what charges they would face. The prosecutor, a man of crude pomposity, Dr Percy Yutar, told the opposing lawyers that a visit to Pretoria Prison would enable them to find out whom they were defending. Presumably he enjoyed what he intended as a joke. It was to be but the first example of his cynical and unprofessional manner.

When at last, on 9 October 1963, the men were herded into the dock of the Palace of Justice in Pretoria, Bram Fischer opened with a devastating attack on the indictment. It was, he said, legally shoddy and so full of outlandish mistakes as to render it absurd. Among a host of inaccuracies, Mandela was charged with crimes he was supposed to have committed while already imprisoned on Robben Island. The Judge-President of the Transvaal, Quartus de Wet, quashed the indictment. However, before there was time to realise that technically the accused were free, Lieutenant Swanepoel, a fanatic in the security police, jumped into the dock and re-arrested each man on the charge of sabotage. In December the trial resumed.

When Mandela first appeared from his three months of solitary confinement his appearance shocked all those who saw him. He had lost almost 40 pounds in weight and his skin had the yellowish tint of prison pallor. His colleagues, too, were drawn and haggard. But Fischer, at the first abortive hearing, had appealed for, and won, better prison conditions for the accused. Now, when they came into the dock, they were transformed, especially Mandela, who wore a well-cut three-piece suit and whose entire demeanour was more confident and assured. The main charges against him were sabotage, being part of a conspiracy to overthrow the government by revolution and assisting in armed invasion of South Africa by foreign troops. The maximum penalty was death. When the Registrar asked him how he pleaded Mandela said, 'The government should be in the dock, not me. I plead not guilty.'

As in Mandela's previous trial, the verdict was a foregone conclusion. The prosecution case, which took five months to present, alleged that the defendants were responsible for 222 acts of sabotage, but that number was reduced to 193. The prosecution's own witnesses testified that the Umkhonto High Command had consistently issued instructions to avoid loss of human life. Yutar was undeterred. Ignoring the outrage of the defending lawyers, he talked of Umkhonto planning 'violent insurrection' against 'the so-called yoke of white domination'; he used the words 'murder' and 'attempted murder' frequently and deliberately. In this atmosphere it was little wonder that Mandela and his companions decided not to contest the charges on strictly legal grounds. They wanted a political trial in which they could castigate the government and make their own beliefs heard in the outside world. It was a brave decision which verged on the reckless. After much argument, accused and their lawyers agreed that the most effective tactic would be for Mandela to make a long political statement from the dock and for Sisulu and the others to submit to cross-examination by the prosecution.

For more than four hours Mandela addressed the court, reading from notes he had prepared over the past weeks. Early in his speech he startled the court and added to the drama:

> ... I must deal immediately, and at some length, with the question of violence. Some of the things so far told the court are true and some are untrue. I do not, however, deny that I planned sabotage. I did not plan it in a spirit of recklessness, nor because I have any love of violence. I planned it as a result of a calm and sober assessment of the political situation that had arisen after many years of tyranny, exploitation and oppression of my people by the whites.
>
> I admit immediately that I was one of the persons who helped to form *Umkhonto we Sizwe* and that I played a prominent role in its affairs until I was arrested in August 1962.

This cool, analytical tone underscored most of what he said. The main thrust of his argument was that Umkhonto had answered violence with violence. In the face of increasing government brutality, the blacks had no other choice. He traced the history of the ANC's policy of non-violence and quoted from Lutuli's Nobel Prize acceptance speech:

What [Lutuli asked] have been the fruits of moderation? The past thirty years have seen the greatest number of laws restricting our rights and progress, until today we have reached a stage where we have almost no rights at all.

Much of Mandela's defence was dominated by his need to respond yet again to accusations of communist influence in the ANC. He was at pains to parry the allegation that the aims of the ANC and the Communist Party were identical:

The ideological creed of the ANC is, and always has been, the creed of African nationalism ... The African nationalism for which the ANC stands, is the concept of freedom and fulfilment for the African people in their own land ...

He explained that the Freedom Charter was by no means a blueprint for a socialist state since it called for redistribution not nationalisation. The ANC had never advocated a revolutionary change in the economic structure of the country, nor had it ever condemned capitalist society. The Communist Party, however, stood for the establishment of a state based on the principles of Marxism. The ANC's chief goal was

for the African people to win unity and full political rights. The Communist Party's main aim, on the other hand, was to remove capitalists and to replace them with a working-class government. The Communist Party sought to emphasize the class distinctions whilst the ANC seeks to harmonize them. This is a vital distinction.

In a brilliant passage he sought to explain that close cooperation between the ANC and the Communist Party was merely proof of a common goal – the removal of white supremacy.

The history of the world is full of similar examples. Perhaps the most striking illustration is to be found in the cooperation between Great Britain, the United States of America and the Soviet Union in the fight against Hitler. Nobody but Hitler would have dared to suggest that such cooperation turned Churchill or Roosevelt into communist tools, or that Britain and America were working to bring about a communist world.

It was precisely this kind of cooperation into which Umkhonto had entered with the communists.

Turning to his own political creed, Mandela said he had always regarded himself, first and foremost, as an African patriot. He admitted freely that he was attracted to the idea of a classless society which sprang in part from

> Marxist reading and, in part, from my admiration of the structure and organization of early African societies in this country. The land, then the main means of production, belonged to the tribe. There were no rich or poor and there was no exploitation.

He also admitted that he had been influenced by Marxist thought, but so, he said, were people as diverse as Ghandi, Nehru, Nkrumah and Nasser. All accepted the need for some form of socialism to enable their people to overcome extreme poverty. But this, he said, did not mean they were Marxists. He went further by saying he thought it debatable whether or not the Communist Party had any specific role to play in this particular stage of the political struggle. The basic task, as he saw it, was the removal of race discrimination and the attainment of democratic rights. In so far as the Communist Party furthered that task, he welcomed its assistance. But he had his reservations:

> ... I have gained the impression that communists regard the parliamentary system of the West as undemocratic and reactionary. But, on the contrary, I am an admirer of such a system ... I have great respect for British political institutions, and for the country's system of justice. I regard the British Parliament as the most democratic institution in the world ... The American Congress, that country's separation of powers, as well as the independence of its judiciary, arouses in me similar sentiments.

In the development of his political thought he had been influenced by West and East. He was eclectic in his search for a formula applicable to South Africa, free to borrow the best ideas wherever they may be found.

Time and again he stressed the Africanism of Umkhonto which, he avowed, had not been inspired by communists or agitators as the State Prosecutor alleged. Indeed, even his travels abroad had been undertaken in order to raise funds from African states. Umkhonto was formed by Africans to further their struggle for freedom in their own land.

> Our fight is against real, and not imaginary, hardships or, to use the language of the State Prosecutor, 'so-called hardships'. Basically, we fight against two features which are the hallmarks of African life in South Africa and which are entrenched by legislation which we seek to have repealed. These features are poverty and lack of human dignity, and we do not need communists or so-called 'agitators' to teach us about these things.

He was entering the home straight, describing in some detail the grinding poverty of blacks, the government's determination to educate them to minimal standards, quoting Verwoerd's infamous intervention in a parliamentary debate in 1953. 'When I have control of Native education', Verwoerd had said, 'I will reform it so that Natives will be taught from childhood to realise that equality with Europeans is not for them.' Mandela lashed into job reservation, the Pass Laws, the breakdown of family life which led inevitably to juvenile delinquency and immorality. He set forth the minimum demands for a living wage, the right to perform any work of which a man or woman was capable, to travel freely, to own property. Above all he demanded equal political rights.

All those present in court listened spellbound to a remarkable performance which combined intellect and passion, a well-reasoned and deeply-felt postulation of political and social ills. In retrospect, his speech on that April day in 1964 is a dramatic reminder of the opportunity that Mandela, and only Mandela, offered the whites. But then the history of South Africa is riddled with missed opportunities. Had the ruling power for one brief moment regarded him as a responsible leader with whom it was possible to deal instead of, at worst, a sub-human, at best, a 'cheeky kaffir' who was only interested in violence and revolution, there may have been another, more inspiring history to record. As it was, the note of true inspiration came from Mandela in his closing, intensely personal and moving statement:

> During my lifetime I have dedicated myself to this struggle of the African people. I have fought against white domination, and I have fought against black domination. I have cherished the ideal of a democratic and free society in which all persons live together in

harmony with equal opportunities. It is an ideal which I hope to live for and to achieve. But if needs be, it is an ideal for which I am prepared to die.

A collective sigh rose from the public gallery as he sat down.

The trial ground on until June. Yutar insisted that guerrilla warfare had been the aim of the accused. The Judge, prodded by the defence, dismissed the allegation. Nevertheless, since Mandela and most of his colleagues had admitted their guilt, the final outcome was never in doubt – except in the case of three of the accused, Kathrada, Bernstein and Mhlaba, who had denied the charges against them. Only one real question, however, remained to be settled: would Mandela, Sisulu and the others be sentenced to death?

Winnie was in court for the verdict. From the gallery she looked down on her husband and his friends, heard all of them, except Bernstein, pronounced guilty. Sentence was to be meted out the following day. Throughout the world men of good will demanded that the death penalty should not be exacted. All sides of the political spectrum appealed for mercy. The *New York Times* called the defendants the George Washingtons and Benjamin Franklins of South Africa. Its editorial was no doubt right in claiming that to most of the world these men were heroes and freedom fighters. Mary Benson, Mandela's biographer, reported the efforts behind the scenes of Bram Fischer who, she wrote,

approached two distinguished South Africans to argue in mitigation: Harold Hanson, QC compared the African struggle for rights to the Afrikaner struggle for freedom and cited precedents for temperate sentencing, even in cases of rebellion and treason; while Alan Paton [author of *Cry, The Beloved Country*], National President of the Liberal Party and a devout Christian, praised the sincerity and courage of Mandela, Sisulu and Mbeki and spoke of their lack of desire for revenge. He appealed for clemency 'because of the future of this country'.

On the following morning, 12 June, the defendants were for the last time taken from their cells and brought into the dock. Outside the large crowd was silent, waiting, praying. Their banners said simply: WE ARE PROUD OF OUR LEADERS and NO TEARS: OUR FUTURE IS BRIGHT. In court the Judge entered and pronounced sentence: life imprisonment. The prisoners turned to their families and friends in the gallery and smiled. Mandela gave the

ANC salute and was taken away. Dennis Goldberg, the only white, was confined in Pretoria Central Prison. Mandela and the others refused to appeal against their sentences and were flown to Robben Island.

Winnie was now alone. With her husband in prison she had to struggle to bring up her two daughters, to make some sort of life for them and for herself. But given the inhuman political system and a vindictive government, her suffering was to be intensified. Prior to Mandela's last trial in 1964, she had been arrested twice and banned for two years under the Suppression of Communism Act. She had spent two weeks in prison. But then, in those years, the authorities had concentrated their might on Mandela himself; now that he was behind bars Winnie became the favourite target. Hardly a year has passed since 1965 when she has not been harassed, restricted, imprisoned, banned, banished, detained, charged, acquitted, re-arrested. No matter where totalitarian governments exist, no matter of what political extreme, they all have one thing in common: a neurotic hatred of the individual. South Africa is no exception. Bringing to bear a kind of clumsy, lumbering cruelty, the state bore down on Winnie Mandela in the hope presumably of breaking her spirit and extinguishing the flame her husband had lit. But the history of the world is full of individuals who cannot be cowed by brute force, who, because of the persecution they suffer, emerge stronger, more defiant, their voices louder than ever and who cannot be silenced except by death. In a way, the South African government itself, by its treatment of Winnie, helped to create the most potent symbol of resistance to its own existence.

FROM THE SCREENPLAY

EXT. SOWETO CEMETERY. DAY
A funeral procession makes its way towards the cemetery and the open graves. Men carry the coffins of children. THE CROWD sing 'Se Nzemi Na?'

ANGLE
The large CROWD surrounds the graves for fifty coffins. After the PRIEST recites a prayer, WINNIE, deeply moved, addresses the crowd.

WINNIE

Amandla! Amandla! Amandla!

CROWD

Ngawethu!

WINNIE

We come today to bury our children,
fifty of them, shot by the police who
opened fire without warning. We cry out
against these killings. What was the
protest in Soweto about? It was about
our children, our little ones, refusing
to learn Afrikaans, the language of the
oppressors. Afrikaans is not their
language, so why must they learn it?
And if they must learn Afrikaans, then
the Prime Minister should learn Zulu.
All over the world men of goodwill fight
for the justice of our cause for the
release of our brothers and sisters from
their prisons. And I bring you messages
of love from our leaders inside those
prisons. I bring you deep sympathies
from the families who share with you
the pain of our country. *Amandla!*

CROWD

Ngawethu!

WINNIE

We are here as testimony to the effect
that the solution to this country's
problems lies in these black hands.
This is our country. In the same way
that you have today had to bury our
loved ones, our children, so shall the
blood of these little heroes we bury
today be avenged. We are here to tell
you that the day is not too far when we
shall lead you to freedom. *Amandla*!

CROWD

Amandla! *Ngawethu*! Free Mandela!
Free Mandela! Free Mandela! Free
Mandela!

10

'I WILL RETURN'

Mandela and his friends, being political prisoners, were classified Category D, which meant they were allowed one letter of 500 words and one half-hour visit every six months. The visits were strictly controlled: no speaking in a 'Bantu' language, no reference to anyone other than children or 'first degree relatives', no discussion of prison conditions; if these rules were broken, visits were abruptly terminated. For Winnie it meant a journey of a 1,000 miles from Orlando, near Johannesburg, to Cape Town. Accompanied by warders she would be shown into a room where her husband waited, separated from her by a glass panel. Physical contact was forbidden; they talked through telephones, their conversations monitored by the warders. When the thirty minutes of stilted, awkward conversation was over, Winnie returned by ferry to Cape Town and made the long journey back to Orlando.

These pathetic biannual 'privileges' were the highlights of the prisoners' year; the rest of their time they existed in appalling conditions, on a bleak and desolate rock which was often shrouded in mist and buffeted by savage winds and seas, their every move supervised by tough, brutal warders.

Like some of the inmates in Solzhenytsin's *Gulag Archipelago*, the political prisoners on Robben Island were made to build their own prison. They helped to erect a special isolation block of eighty-eight cells separated from the criminal fraternity by a thirty-foot wall. Mandela's cell, like the others, was approximately seven foot square and lit by a single 40-watt bulb. He slept on the floor on a mat with two inadequate blankets for cover. The food was tasteless, repetitive and lacked nourishment. Inexplicably, the Indian and Coloured prisoners were allowed a spoonful of sugar and bread with some meals; the Africans were given half a spoonful of sugar but no bread. To begin with they were forbidden exercise and were locked all day in their cells. Mandela complained and in time won his first small victory: the politicals were put out in the yard to break stones. Although talking to each other was an offence, they still somehow managed to communicate.

118

In summer they worked in the lime quarry. Chained together by the ankles, they were marched in pairs to the centre of the island. It was a cruel place. The work was back-breaking and the sun beat down relentlessly, the lime acting as a monstrous reflector intensifying the heat and the glare. At midday the quarry was a blast-furnace. By the time the exhausted men returned to their cells in late afternoon, they were covered in limedust and looked like spectres, weary inhabitants of a man-made purgatory.

So the years passed. The authorities tried every means of breaking the men's morale. But Mandela and Sisulu knew that survival depended on preserving their own dignity and integrity; they were an inspiration to their fellow-prisoners. Mandela complained against conditions, was punished, refused to obey orders, was put in solitary, released, and then continued his complaints. Helen Suzman, the Progressive Party MP, demanded to see him and was eventually given permission. To her Mandela complained of one particular warder who had visited him in his cell. The man had rolled up his sleeve and shown Mandela a swastika tattooed on his forearm. 'These are my politics', the warder said, 'and you're going to pay for them.' On her return she took up the matter with the appropriate Minister and the warder was removed. These and other victories nourished survival.

Perhaps the most important privilege gained was the right to study. Mandela furthered his legal knowledge. When the men met together they exchanged information, each contributing from their own specialised subject. Although the prisoners were not allowed newspapers, they somehow managed to pick up scraps of news. Indeed, press clippings were found hidden in Mandela's cell for which he was punished. Often the authorities made certain that the prisoners heard about an event that would be sure to upset them: an arrest, a death, a setback for the struggle. In Mandela's particular case, he was always at his most vulnerable when told of what was happening to Winnie. So the years passed.

In 1965, a year after Mandela's trial, Winnie was banned for five years and restricted to Orlando Township. As a result she lost her job with the Child Welfare Society. In 1966 the government imposed additional restrictions which prevented her from 'preparing, compiling, publishing, printing or transmitting any document, book, pamphlet, record, poster, photograph' and more or less anything else dreamed up by the authorities. Police harassment was constant. One day, in 1967, a Sergeant Fourie paid her a visit and entered her house without knocking. She described to Anne Benjamin what happened:

> I was in my bedroom. I had my skirt half-way up – heavens! – and he walked in like that, he didn't retreat and say 'excuse me'; he finds me standing in this humiliating position in the bedroom and he continues as if I'm just a piece of furniture! And then he puts his hand on my shoulder! I don't know how he landed on his neck. All I remember is grabbing him, and throwing him on the floor, which is what he deserved. I remember seeing his legs up in the air and him screaming, and the whole dressing-stand falling on him. This is how he broke his neck (he did recover).

She was arrested, charged with assault but found not guilty and acquitted. Anyone who came into contact with her or tried to help in the upbringing and education of her children was immediately suspect and subject to vicious treatment by the security police. The government, it seems, was determined to shatter her spirit and to remove from African consciousness the Mandela name or, at the very least, to debase and tarnish it. Insinuations that she was having illicit love affairs were frequent. 'MAN FOUND IN MANDELA'S HOUSE' the headlines screamed, but these attacks had little effect, and so in 1969 the state was driven to more extreme action.

There was by then a new Prime Minister and his succession was the result of a drama played out three years before in the House of Assembly. On the afternoon of 6 September 1966, just before the Speaker's procession entered the chamber at 2.15 p.m., division bells as usual rang to summon members to their seats. During these few minutes parliamentary messengers are permitted in the chamber and there was much activity on the floor. The public galleries were packed because the Prime Minister, Dr Verwoerd, was due to answer his opposition critics in debate. Wives of Cabinet Ministers and members were in their specially reserved seats. The bays reserved for the diplomatic corps and for guests of the Prime Minister and the Speaker were also full. On the front bench sat the Minister of Justice, B. J. Vorster, and the Minister of Defence, P. W. Botha. Presently, Dr Verwoerd entered, had a word with his Chief Whip and sat down. As he did so a white man in parliamentary messenger's uniform entered the chamber from the lobby and moved towards Verwoerd. He bent over the Prime Minister, raising his right hand high in the air. He was holding a sheath knife. With his left hand he plucked off the sheath and plunged the knife downwards. Verwoerd fell back but remained sitting upright for a moment before collapsing. The messenger continued to stab Verwoerd several times before he was pulled away and disarmed. The messenger's name was Dimitri Stafendas and he was later found to be insane. Ironically, there was no political motive. The Apostle of Apartheid, venerated by his supporters, despised by his enemies, died at the hands of a madman. Exactly a week later the Nationalist Party caucus voted for a new leader, the pro-Nazi Minister of Justice, B. J. Vorster.

By 1969 Vorster was well established in power which, according to an American observer, Arnold Beichmann, he exuded 'like some men exude money ... He is a man who gives the impression that he is in full control and nothing can swing him from his course.' From the start of his premiership Vorster ruthlessly pursued his opponents white and black. 'If I see a man or a woman as a threat to the State', he had said, 'and if there are valid reasons for not bringing that person to trial, then I must take them out of circulation one way or another.' One of the ways he sought to take people out of circulation was under the Terrorism Act of 1967, which enabled the police to arrest any person suspected of committing acts endangering the maintenance of law and order or conspiring or inciting people to commit such acts. The Act was so loosely drawn that Vorster and his cohorts could hold anyone they chose without a warrant, detaining them for interrogation in solitary confinement without access to a lawyer or relative for an indefinite period. Children were not exempted. Under these provisions, at 2 a.m. on 12 May 1969, the first arrests were made. Twenty-two people were detained, among them Winnie Mandela. She was to spend 491 days in detention, most of the time in solitary confinement.

Those eighteen months in solitary put the steel into Winnie's soul. She had once remarked that suffering was a prerequisite of struggle. Her suffering in a South African jail gave physical meaning to her beliefs, far more satisfying, she said later, than articulating them from a platform. 'When you are inside, you know why you are there and the people who put you there also know.'

She was held in Pretoria Central Prison: it is difficult to imagine a crueller regime. Kept in a small cell, at first she did not know there were other detainees in the same block. All she was given was a sanitary bucket, a plastic bottle with enough water for three glasses, and a mug. During menstruation she was told to use toilet paper, or the white wardress would say, 'Go and use your big fat hands.' The days were endless. She talked to herself, stood, sat, paced. She remembered finding two ants and playing with them on her finger all day. A light was kept burning in her cell at night. Sleep was impossible. But worse was to come.

Interrogation began two weeks after her arrest. Her tormentor-in-chief was Major Swanepoel, one of the most notorious members of the Security Police, against whom many allegations of torture had been made. She was kept awake for five days and nights and questioned continuously by relays of interrogators. By the third day her hands and feet were swollen; she was dizzy and suffering from heart palpitations. Swanepoel, like a caricature SS officer, said, 'For God's sake, leave us some inheritance when you decide to pop it. You can't go with all that information.'

Fellow prisoners were tortured more severely. Some were suspended by their wrists and beaten; others were made to stand in their bare feet on bricks until they collapsed and then forced to continue the exercise. The laughter of interrogators was often heard. In totalitarian states there is never a shortage of sadists.

Winnie endured a first spell of solitary confinement for five months before being brought to trial with twenty-one others in Pretoria's old synagogue. All had been held under the Terrorism Act but were now charged under the Suppression of Communism Act on a variety of alleged offences which included recruiting for the ANC, identifying targets for sabotage and distributing banned literature. Winnie was also charged with carrying messages from her imprisoned husband. Behind the government's action was the real fear that the ANC was experiencing a revival. Many witnesses – most of whom were detainees – refused to testify and as a result suffered further imprisonment, but the evidence in any case against Winnie and the others was so pathetic that the state was forced to ask for their acquittal. They were found not guilty and discharged, but, as though living a recurring nightmare, they were immediately re-arrested and again detained under the Terrorism Act. Winnie found herself back in solitary and facing her interrogators. Later, in a filmed interview, she said:

> I have been so hardened by this experience that, at the end of my interrogation, if my own father walked in dangling a gun, and if he was on the other side, then, if I had a gun, too, in defence of the ideals for which I was being tortured, I would fire.

Abroad, the protests mounted against her treatment. The government's strategy of holding men and women under the Terrorism Act until sufficient evidence could be obtained or invented was so transparent that the prosecution was finally obliged to bring the accused once more to court. On 14 September 1970 they were acquitted for the second time. A month later Winnie was subjected to a stricter ban

– virtual house arrest – under which, amongst other things, she was allowed no visitors. The authorities were so intent on harassing her that when she became ill and was visited by her sister, Winnie was arrested for breaking this latest banning order.

For Mandela, the long months of Winnie's incarceration were his torture. He could get little news of her and, of course, she was not allowed to write to him. It was during this period that another tragedy blighted his life. His son from his first marriage was killed in a motor car accident. But 1970 ended on a brighter note. Winnie was given special permission to leave Orlando and she set off for Robben Island. It was the first time husband and wife had been in each other's presence for two years.

Mandela kept himself politically active even on the island. He drafted a petition calling for the release of political prisoners and, occasionally, saw distinguished visitors from the mainland – Helen Suzman, for example. The Minister of Prisons, Jimmy Kruger, appeared and, in an effort to gain approval for the government's policy of 'Bantustans', offered a deal. If Mandela would recognise and live in the Transkei, where he was born, there would be a remission of sentence. Mandela declined the offer. And although he had won a great many privileges for himself and his companions over the years, he was still forced to labour, now put to collecting seaweed for fertilisers. His days were spent at the water's edge, harnessed to his fellows like oxen, their legs immersed in the icy Atlantic.

In spite of a constant police watch on her every movement, Winnie continued to behave with courage and dignity. In 1974 she was sentenced to six months in prison, again for breaking her banning order. The authorities cracked down on her so frequently that she herself cannot recall the details. It was as if she were waging a one-woman defiance campaign against injustice, her husband's imprisonment, the entire apparatus of apartheid. Then, unexpectedly, her bans ran out and, inexplicably, were not renewed. She was free to travel, address meetings, give interviews to the press. For someone who had been so much confined, so cut off from contact with the outside world, she revealed a telling insight and prophesied tragedy: young blacks, she warned, were filled with anger; one day they would take their revenge on the system that brutalised them.

The schoolchildren of Soweto, 15,000 of them, converged on Orlando West Junior Secondary School on the morning of 16 June 1976. They were protesting against being forced to do their studies

in Afrikaans. DOWN WITH AFRIKAANS! their banners screamed,
WE ARE NOT BOERS! and IF WE MUST DO AFRIKAANS,
VORSTER MUST DO ZULU! They also demanded the release of
Mandela, Sisulu and other political prisoners. The marchers were
confronted by a hastily summoned and aggressive police detachment
who tried to disperse the children with tear gas. When that failed, the
police fired into the crowd, killing two and injuring several more. Tom
Lodge takes up the story:

> The schoolchildren retreated and fanned out into the township.
> By midday rioting had broken out in several parts of Soweto; cars
> were stoned and barricades erected, arson attacks took place on
> administration buildings and beer halls, and two white men were
> attacked and killed. The rioting continued into the evening and
> deepened in intensity when police baton-charged crowds of com-
> muters outside railway stations.

Four days of rioting followed and the death toll mounted. According
to official figures 176 died and at least 1,800 were injured. The
violence spread to other parts of the country. The anger which Winnie
had identified was now unleashed on the police and army. The only
responsible body in Soweto was the Black Parents Association, of
which Winnie was a leader. They organised the grim task of identifying and burying the dead children. At the funeral of fifty-nine of them,
Winnie gave the valediction, an impassioned lament recorded by a
newsreel camera:

> In the same way that you have had to bury our loved ones today,
> our children, so shall the blood of these little heroes we bury today
> be avenged. We are here to tell you that the day is not far off when
> we shall lead you to freedom. *Amandla!*

The violence and protests lasted for more than a year. There was
a national boycott of schools and the death toll soared. The actual
number of dead will never be known, but it is certain that at least 700
died, more probably 1,000. The students' ranks were decimated and
they found it hard to regroup and keep up the momentum. The revolt
of the children – which came near to a full-scale rebellion – fizzled
out.

Winnie was punished, along with many others, by a five-month term
of imprisonment. Later, in May 1977, in the early hours of the morning, twenty policemen burst into her Soweto house and served an

order banishing her for seven years to a town called Brandfort in the Orange Free State. A wag described Brandfort as a one-horse town without a horse. To the 'native' location in this miserable spot, she and her daughter, Zindzi, with some of their possessions, were driven by the police. The timing was significant: a week later President Carter was sending the United States Ambassador to the United Nations, Andrew Young, on a visit to Soweto. To Anne Benjamin Winnie said, 'I am of no importance to them as an individual. What I stand for is what they want to banish. I couldn't think of a greater honour.'

It was not enough for the government to banish her to a hovel 300 miles from Johannesburg. Each night, at weekends and on public holidays she was placed under house arrest. Only one person could visit her at a time. The police watched her wherever she went. Even so, once she had overcome the terrible shock of her uprooting, she set about organising help for the poverty-stricken inhabitants of the location who were now her neighbours. Her training as a social worker enabled her to cope with dreadful cases of malnutrition, to help pregnant mothers, to care for the younger children whose parents had to work from dawn till dusk.

That year, 1977, saw the renewal of the armed struggle. The guerrillas and saboteurs filtered back across the border into South Africa. An ANC recruit, Solomon Mahlangu, was captured. He was involved in an incident in which white men had been killed, although he himself had not fired a shot. He was brought to trial and sentenced to death. The widow of one of the dead men joined in the worldwide protests, but the government remained intractable. Mahlangu was hanged.

On 18 July 1978 Mandela celebrated his sixtieth birthday. He had so far spent sixteen years in prison. His name was becoming known to a wider public and his plight beginning to concern people in all parts of the world. Somehow, through enormous reserves of strength and fortitude, he had survived and survived well. He was physically fit and amazingly well informed. To his wife he wrote, 'Had it not been for your visits, wonderful letters and your love, I would have fallen apart many years ago.'

Corruption brought down B. J. Vorster. Financial scandal involving a member of his cabinet, Dr Mulder, forced the Prime Minister's resignation in 1978. He was succeeded by a party *apparatchik*, P. W. Botha, a dull, unimaginative man of whom Helen Suzman said, 'No,

I would not describe P. W. as an intellectual.' Nevertheless, his leadership would see a shift in Afrikaner thought, an apparent move towards a more enlightened society. He made himself State President – head of state and chief executive combined. His tinkering with the system, parliamentary and social, would fool only those who hoped he could maintain in some form the *status quo*. His policy was the carrot and the whip: limited reforms to appease his left wing and world opinion; repression to appease his right. It was not for humanitarian reasons that Botha instituted change but because apartheid had proved in every way, especially economically, an unmitigated disaster. World opinion had its effect, albeit a limited one. The *laager* mentality of the Afrikaner could still be counted on to defend white supremacy. 'We do not need foreigners to tell us how to run our country', Botha said. For the people most affected, the non-whites, his policies had little to offer. Their indifference to the government's actions was summed up by Mandela after the abolition of the Immorality Act. It was of no interest to him, he said, since he had no intention of marrying a white woman.

1980 saw the start in earnest of the FREE MANDELA campaign, which was to gather an unstoppable momentum. Even white students in South Africa itself cried out for his release. In Brandfort Winnie received, one by one, Western journalists, and kept the flame burning. Vigils were held outside South African embassies; streets and buildings were named after him; hardly a day passed without his name being mentioned in newspapers, on radio and television. Mandela and South Africa had at last entered the consciousness of the world community.

Out of the blue Mandela was moved from Robben Island. The reasons have never been clear but in April 1982 he, Sisulu, Kathrada, Mhlaba and Mlangeni – all Rivonia men – were abruptly taken to the mainland, to Pollsmoor Maximum Security Prison near Cape Town. A sympathetic warder from the island, Sergeant Gregory, accompanied them. Conditions were marginally better. Mandela and his companions were confined to a dormitory cell but because of a high wall they could see nothing of one of the most beautiful landscapes in the world. This was a particular hardship for Mandela, who once told a visitor he now understood what Oscar Wilde had meant by the phrase 'the little tent of blue that prisoners call the sky'. Winnie was allowed monthly visits but she and her husband were still separated by glass and communicated through microphones.

Suddenly those conditions were also changed. In May 1984 Winnie arrived with Zeni and her baby daughter at Pollsmoor for a routine visit. They were met by Sergeant Gregory who called them into an office. Immediately Winnie thought her husband was ill. 'As from now on', Gregory said, 'you will be able to have different visits. I thought I should bring the news gently to you.' Mandela was led in. They kissed and she held him for a long time. It was their first physical contact for twenty-two years.

It is an experience one just can't put into words [Winnie said]. It was fantastic and hurting at the same time. He clung to the child right through the visit. Gregory ... was so moved, he looked the other way.

There is no final act in the saga of Nelson and Winnie Mandela. While he remains in prison and the present system of government in his country continues, they are trapped in the circumstances of a tragic history, participants in an unfolding drama, symbolic figures in a struggle for human dignity. To the white rulers of South Africa they are like sores that will not heal, constant reminders of the illness that infects the body politic. Their longing to be rid of Mandela, to find some formula which may consign him to obscurity, was revealed in 1985, on 31 January, when P. W. Botha made an announcement in the House of Assembly:

The government is willing to consider Mr Mandela's release in the Republic of South Africa on condition that Mr Mandela gives a commitment that he will not make himself guilty of planning, instigating or committing acts of violence for the furtherance of political objectives ... It is therefore not the South African government which now stands in the way of Mr Mandela's freedom. It is he himself. The choice is his. All that is required of him now is that he should unconditionally reject violence as a political instrument. This is, after all, a norm which is respected in all civilized countries of the world.

Mandela replied a week later. In the presence of Winnie and their lawyer, Ismail Ayob, Mandela began to dictate his statement. Prison personnel tried to stop him; Mandela suggested they telephone the State President for further instructions; he was allowed to continue with his message. He would have liked Winnie to read his words to the people but she, being banned, was forbidden to address public meetings. In her place, Zindzi stood before a vast crowd in the

Jabulani amphitheatre in Soweto. Winnie was on the platform to hear her daughter read Mandela's response to Botha's offer:

My father and his comrades wish to make this statement to you, the people, first. They are clear that they are accountable to you and to you alone. And that you should hear their views directly and not through others.

My father speaks not only for himself and for his comrades at Pollsmoor Prison but he hopes he also speaks for all those in jail for their opposition to apartheid, for all those who are banished, for all those who are in exile, for all those who suffer under apartheid, for all those who are opponents of apartheid and for all those who are oppressed and exploited. Throughout our struggle there have been puppets who have claimed to speak for you. They have made this claim, both here and abroad. They are of no consequence. My father and his colleagues will not be like them.

My father says, 'I am a member of the African National Congress. I have always been a member of the African National Congress and I will remain a member of the African National Congress until the day I die. Oliver Tambo is much more than a brother to me. He is my greatest friend and comrade for nearly fifty years. If there is any one among you who cherishes my freedom, Oliver Tambo cherishes it more, and I know that he would give his life to see me free. There is no difference betwen his views and mine.'

My father says, 'I am surprised at the conditions that the government wants to impose on me. I am not a violent man. My colleagues and I wrote in 1952 to Malan asking for a round table conference to find a solution to the problems of our country but that was ignored.

'When Strijdom was in power, we made the same offer. Again it was ignored.

'When Verwoerd was in power we asked for a National Convention for all the people in South Africa to decide on their future. This, too, was in vain.

'It was only then when all other forms of resistance were no longer open to us that we turned to armed struggle.

'Let Botha show that he is different to Malan, Strijdom and Verwoerd. Let him renounce violence. Let him say that he will dismantle apartheid.

'Let him unban the people's organization, the African National

Congress. Let him free all who have been imprisoned, banished or exiled for their opposition to apartheid. Let him guarantee free political activity so that the people may decide who may govern them.

'I cherish my own freedom dearly but I care even more for your freedom. Too many have died since I went to prison. Too many have suffered for the love of freedom. I owe it to their widows, to their orphans, to their mothers and to their fathers who have grieved and wept for them. Not only I have suffered during these long lonely wasted years. I am not less life-loving than you are. But I cannot sell my birthright nor am I prepared to sell the birthright of the people to be free. I am in prison as the representative of the people and of your organization, the African National Congress, which was banned. What freedom am I being offered while the organization of the people remains banned? What freedom am I being offered when I may be arrested on a pass offence? What freedom am I being offered to live my life as a family with my dear wife who remains in banishment in Brandfort? What freedom am I being offered when I must ask for permission to live in an urban area? What freedom am I being offered when I need a stamp in my pass to seek work? What freedom am I being offered when my very South African citizenship is not respected?

'Only free men can negotiate. Prisoners cannot enter into contracts. Herman Toivo Ja Toivo, when freed, never gave any undertaking, nor was he called upon to do so.'

My father says, 'I cannot and will not give any undertaking at a time when I and you, the people, are not free. Your freedom and mine cannot be separated. I will return.'

The rest will be history.

SELECT BIBLIOGRAPHY

ATTWELL, Michael, *South Africa, Background to the Crisis*, Sidgwick & Jackson, London, 1986

BENSON, Mary, *Nelson Mandela, The Man and the Movement*, W. W. Norton & Co., New York and London, 1986

——,*The African Patriots*, Faber, London, 1963

COMAROFF, John L. (ed.), *The Boer War Diary of Sol T. Plaatje*, Macmillan, London, 1973

D'OLIVEIRA, *Vorster – The Man*, Ernest Stanton, Johannesburg, 1977

ELLIOTT, Aubrey, *The Magic World of the Xhosa*, Collins, London, 1970

FIRST, Ruth, *117 Days*, Penguin, London, 1982

GILBERT, Martin, *The Holocaust*, Collins, London, 1986

HARRISON, David, *The White Tribe of Africa*, BBC, London, 1981

HARRISON, Nancy, *Winnie Mandela, Mother of a Nation*, Grafton, London, 1986

HUDDLESTON, Trevor, *Naught for Your Comfort*, Collins, London, 1956

JOSEPH, Helen, *If This Be Treason*, André Deutsch, London, 1963

LELYVELD, Joseph, *Move Your Shadow*, Michael Joseph, London, 1986

LODGE, Tom, *Black Politics in South Africa since 1945*, Longman, London, 1983

LUTULI, Albert, *Let My People Go*, Collins, London, 1962

MANDELA, Nelson, *The Struggle is my Life*, IDAF, London, 1978

——, *No Easy Walk to Freedom*, Heinemann, London, 1983

MANDELA, Winnie (ed. Anne Benjamin), *Part of my Soul Went with Him*, W. W. Norton & Co., New York and London, 1984

OMOND, Roger, *The Apartheid Handbook*, Penguin, London, 1985

PAKENHAM, Thomas, *The Boer War*, Weidenfeld & Nicolson, London, 1979

PATON, Alan, *Hofmeyr*, OUP, Cape Town, 1965

SAMPSON, Anthony, *The Treason Cage*, Heinemann, London, 1955

TROUP, Freda, *South Africa: An Historical Introduction*, Eyre Methuen, London, 1972

INDEX

131